disorder through each of her children's personal journey. She has us look at the effects on the family system—those you love, those you touch, and the community that surrounds you. The wisdom Melody shares will help you find the strength to believe that no matter what crosses your path in life, you are not alone—not even when lightning strikes twice.

—Catherine Cameron, Psychotherapist

Advance praise for *When Lightning Strikes Twice*

Melody Leclair and her family have created a very informative and beautifully written series of memoirs regarding their journey dealing with mental health issues. If you are a person struggling with a bipolar diagnosis, a family member or friend trying to support a loved one in need, or a professional who works with children and adolescents, read this book! The Leclairs' candid thoughts and personal experiences will help you learn more about bipolar disorders and how to get help. Thank you for writing this amazing book, Melody! Also, thank you, Josée and Luke, for teaching me what being bipolar is like from a first person perspective.

—Karen Kelly-Miller, Teacher

This is a beautiful book. It is an honest, raw, and brave telling of one family's experience with mental health challenges. The writing is accessible and natural. I think right now, more than ever, this is an important story. Reading about how this family and all who supported them came together to navigate the complex and unpredictable world of supporting children with mental health issues was eye-opening. As an educator, I have been part of this process quite a few times and the journey is not for the faint of heart. I am proud of the Leclair family for sharing their experience so openly. The book is informative, funny, captivating, and inspiring! Bravo!

—Heather Walker, Teacher

Melody's book is a prophetic sharing of sacred story that every one of us needs to read. Through exquisite vulnerability, Melody offers us an in-depth journey into the darkness and light of mental illness within a family. *When Lightning Strikes Twice* provides a powerful opportunity for each of us to grow in understanding and the experience of suffering, struggle, grace, compassion, healing, love, joy, and transformation. I am deeply grateful to Melody and all of the people who shared their experiences in the making of this book. We, the readers, are deeply blessed to receive the bountiful harvest from the challenging journey of Melody's family.

—April Snider, Spiritual Director

This book is a beautiful and holy gift for you to open and treasure. In its pages is the authentic story of a family that must change to deal with new realities. It is a story that can change the world. Their story can help to reduce the stigma around mental health. It is a raw story yet so filled with hope. As we follow this family through the tough issues that they face, we are drawn into a bigger human story of loss, of hope, and eventually of new life.

—Debra Nicholson-Elwell, Pastor

Melody's deep sense of love and her amazing strength have carried her and her children through the real world of the heart-breaking and heart-warming story she shares in this book. As a teacher closely associated with her children, I marvel at how she has supported and cared for each of them, and how she has shaped three wonderfully caring, genuine, and compassionate young people despite the struggles placed before all of them. This is a remarkable story.

—Joel Barr, Teacher

Melody knows whereof she speaks. The mother of two children who both had early onset of complicated mental illness, she tells the story of their family with humour and humility. Her vulnerability and authenticity reassure the reader who is struggling with similar issues, and promotes understanding and empathy in those who aren't walking that road themselves but may know someone who is. As a care provider herself, she has the knowledge base to provide accurate information but does so in a format and language that are easy to understand. Her words of guidance for those who are living a similar story are helpful without being prescriptive. I would highly recommend this for any person who has children with mental illness in their world, whether among family or friends, in the classroom or congregation.

—Jan Young Baker, M.D.

When Lightning Strikes Twice is a masterpiece in navigating the mental health maze of the unthinkable, unbelievable, and untouchable. Melody brilliantly and sensitively opens our eyes to the uniqueness of bipolar

WHEN
LIGHTNING
STRIKES
TWICE

One Family's Experience
when Siblings are Diagnosed
with Bipolar Disorder

MELODY LECLAIR

WHEN LIGHTNING STRIKES TWICE
Copyright © 2018 by Melody Leclair

Disclaimer: This is the author's family's account of life with mental illness. It is their hope that their experiences, and the informational appendices that follow it, will encourage others to seek professional diagnosis and treatment. This book is not medical advice or a substitute for it. Everyone's experience with systems is different and wait times or level of service may vary.

Scripture quotations marked (NLT) are taken from the Holy Bible, New Living Translation, copyright ©1996, 2004, 2015 by Tyndale House Foundation. Used by permission of Tyndale House Publishers, Inc., Carol Stream, Illinois 60188. All rights reserved. Scripture quotations marked (NIV) are taken from the Holy Bible, New International Version®, NIV®. Copyright © 1973, 1978, 1984, 2011 by Biblica, Inc.™ Used by permission of Zondervan. All rights reserved worldwide. www.zondervan.com The "NIV" and "New International Version" are trademarks registered in the United States Patent and Trademark Office by Biblica, Inc.™

ISBN: 978-1-4866-1756-2

Word Alive Press
119 De Baets Street, Winnipeg, MB R2J 3R9
www.wordalivepress.ca

WORD ALIVE
—P R E S S—

Cataloguing in Publication may be obtained through Library and Archives Canada.

CONTENTS

ACKNOWLEDGEMENTS

We owe credit to Deb McKelvey Briggs' practice, Let's Talk, for the many years of speech therapy given to both Josée and Luke; Cathy Cameron, a therapist who supplied both one-to-one counselling and family support over the years, as well as time-specific group therapy for Luke to teach him appropriate social skills; Mrs. Karen Kelly-Miller, Luke's fourth and fifth grade teacher, who worked diligently with him to maximize the use of technology and understand his beautiful mind; resource teacher Mrs. Reeds, who encouraged me to get Luke assessed for ADHD; I remember her saying, "You think you are frustrated, so how do you think your son feels?"; Dr. Barr, Josée's audiologist, and the Fast Forward program that helped train Josée's eye-ear-brain coordination skills; Dr. Promnitz, Luke's pediatrician, who assessed him for ADHD; psychologist Dianna Gamble, who performed the kids' psycho-educational assessments; psychiatrist Dr. Edwards for her care, compassion, and ongoing involvement; teacher Joel Barr from CELP (Community Environmental Leadership Program), who visited Luke in hospital and set him up with a peer mentor; the Canadian Mental Health Association; the Grade Nine LAUNCH *Learning* program (Leading Advanced Understanding through Connected Hands-on Learning) and teachers Chris van Beurden and Kelly McCullough; Vice Principal Joe Burns who, according to Luke, demonstrates active listening and spent the time it took to get the kids' supports in place when in and out of hospitals; the hospital nurses, social workers, psychiatrists, and child and youth workers like Kiel, who are good at what they do and work tirelessly and with great compassion to see patients through their treatment process, not to mention extraordinary teachers like Mrs. Walker, Josée's Grade Eight teacher and mother of her friend Emma, who assisted her in her greatest time of crisis and need; Mr. Lyle, who kicked Luke's butt to achieve and not use any of his labels as a crutch; Bill Bulmer, in-school child and youth worker; Miss Cool, for her guidance and help in course selection; Jeff Bershe, MADE (Music, Art, Drama, English) teacher and neighbour; and the extraordinary Sarah Gabriel, who taught Josée's Grade Ten CELP.

We offer further acknowledgements and gratitude to friends and family and to all the contributors both in real life those represented in the book. Special thanks to all those who made the book possible throughout the publication process, and notably our dedicated editor, Sara Davison.

INTRODUCTION

In the spring of 2017, I attended a dialectical behavioural therapy workshop. Afterwards, I approached the facilitator, Sheri Van Dijk, who has written seven books on emotional regulation and by and large works in a hospital setting with patients with borderline personality disorder and bipolar disorder. I informed her of our family situation—raising siblings with bipolar—and asked if she had any experience working with other families like ours, or whether she knew of any applicable resources. Her response incited me to write about our situation, and I declared that intention to her. Others within earshot applauded my assertion with a wink, smile, and a "You go, girl" attitude. Their encouragement, along with my determination to share my family's story, has inspired me to carry out the intention I declared that day.

Bipolar is a mood disorder characterized by extreme highs and lows—and for some, mixed states in between. The symptoms range from feeling too much to too little, or nothing at all. At its peak, mania produces a state of overdrive and sometimes psychosis, while its counterpart evokes feelings of hopelessness and often suicidality, all unwelcome companions. Depending on the severity, those who struggle with the disorder may lack insight about their need for help. In most cases, medication, counselling, and maintaining a healthy lifestyle are essential to achieving a healthy balance and peace of mind.

This book is our family's attempt to share what we are learning about living with mental illness. Although our focus is on bipolar disorder, because that is our personal experience, the book also relates to other forms of mental illness and how a family can be impacted by it and cope. We have written the book together, but for simplicity and clarity the story is told primarily by me (Melody) while the perspectives of friends and family members, as well as a clinician, are identified and interwoven throughout.

It is our hope that telling our story will create awareness of the joys and struggles of our situation, while inciting empathy and compassion for caregivers and others going though similar experiences. We also hope the book will provide helpful tools and possibly serve as a humble guide during those times when it is difficult to know what step to take next. Please note that it is written from raw, undone, heartfelt places and provides candid perspectives and reflections while in the midst of crisis. We have not yet arrived. Our journey from a place of brokenness and struggle to ultimate triumph continues.

Without further ado, here is our story.

A man is walking down the street, and he falls down a hole. He yells for help. A doctor walks by, sees the man, writes a prescription, throws it down the hole, and keeps walking. Later, a priest walks by, sees the man, writes down a prayer, throws it in the hole, and keeps walking. Then a friend walks by, sees the man, and jumps down the hole with him. The man says, "What did you do that for? Now we're both stuck." The friend replies, "Yeah, but I've been down here before, and I know the way out."[1]

—Julia Nunes and Scott Simmie

---

1   Julia Nunes and Scott Simmie, *Beyond Crazy* (Toronto, ON: McClelland & Stewart, 2002), 270.

1. AND THEN IT HIT ME

Luke

I LIE RESTLESS WHILE MY THOUGHTS CARRY ME AWAY TO UNIMAGINABLE places. My mind races as though someone is channel surfing, only there's no remote control that can stop it.

I sit up, I get out of bed, I lie back down, and the cycle continues for hours. Ten o'clock passes, then midnight, 3:30 a.m.... time abounds.

Maybe if I just write things down, getting the thoughts out of my head will stop them. I start to write, theories of everything and why things are the way they are. Such clarity, such genius. If only everyone knew what I knew, the world's problems would be solved. Page after page, I write. Only the more I write, the faster my thoughts come, like a treadmill in high gear, a cruel joke, my thoughts, they haunt me.

I run upstairs to tell my mom I cannot sleep. In a dozy state, she tells me to try harder. I persist. She finally tells me to lie with her and that she has to get up for work in the morning. I lie down, roll over, sit up, and get up again.

I return to my frenzied writing state. My determination to outrace my thoughts persists. I will beat this! I will myself back to bed...

And then it hits me. First a flicker, then a bang. I bolt out of bed and let out a blood-curdling scream: "I have been struck by lightning!" My mom and sisters wake.

"Shut up," Karina yells. "We're trying to sleep."

I frantically tell my mother, the only person who will listen, that I've been struck by lightning, explaining the surge of energy that's pulsating throughout my body, making my heart pound, causing sweat to come out of every pore. I am terrified. Electrified.

I proceed to become over-concerned for the safety of our neighbours, whose house I think was also struck. I drag my mother onto the front porch in her pyjamas and point out the broken hydro pole that has split into multiple pieces. I explain how part of the pole landed on the neighbours' roof, while another part hit and damaged our trailer before landing in the deep window well of the basement near my bedroom.

"I have post-traumatic stress disorder," I exclaim. "I need to be taken to the hospital right away."

The shock is setting in.

Upon arrival at Guelph General, the normally lengthy process of triage and evaluation by the ER medical team is expedited based on the seriousness of my situation. I repeat my situation over and over like a broken record.

I watch as my mother sits quietly in the waiting room for the next eight hours while I, along with nurses and doctors, fervently try to ease my pain of body and mind. I lie in bed, restless. I question every action and inaction. I call to my mother, wanting and rejecting any comfort she has to offer.

Moments of clarity, confusion, and pain continue for the next several hours. Blood work, medication, and observation ensue.

Alas, my father arrives. He's apprehensive; I can sense his fear and concern. He listens as I share my pain, and at points he laughs out loud with his well-known nervous laughter, trying to process all that has happened. That fuels my erratic state. My diagnosis is well suspected.

My parents sit and support one another while talking with various members of my medical team. I can read emotionless, stunned, reluctant relief on their faces. As they approach me, reality begins to break. The doctor validates my experience and proceeds to inform me that he'll be transferring me to a hospital for advanced treatment.

"For what?" I ask.

The doctor replies, "Bipolar disorder. You're in a manic state."

"Bipolar disorder. How can that be? My sister Josée has bipolar, not me."

They don't know what they're talking about. I've been struck by lightning and am suffering from situational PTSD. The only thing we agree on is that I need help.

The next thing I recall, I'm being sedated before being transferred by ambulance to the Child and Adolescent Inpatient Program (CAIP) at Grand River General Hospital in Kitchener. My dad oversees the preparation as I'm strapped into the transfer bed and car.

My mother leaves, unable to bear the sight.

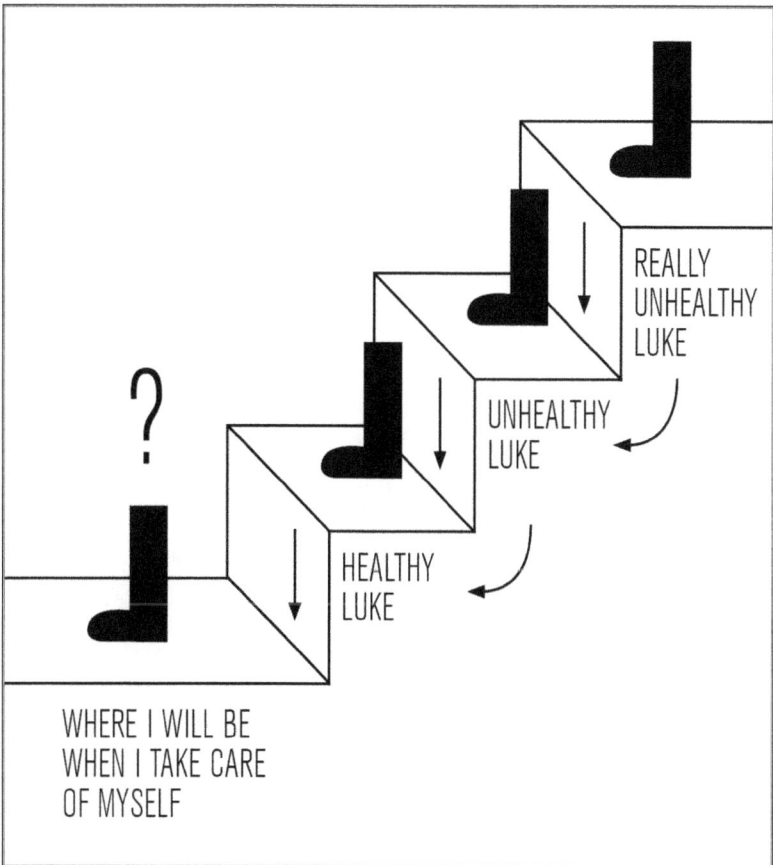

Examples of Luke's manic writings and drawings.

Make a Wish

Whether it is blowing out candles on a cake,
wishing upon a star, picking a four-leaf clover, or
blowing out a dandelion, all in the given hope of
carrying out a wish to be further granted. The
thought that there is something there looking
out for us somehow relieves the pressure.
If there is something out there that will
determine our fate instead of us. They say
create the kind of life you want for yourself, but
maybe you are not supposed to. So, you hope in
superficial things. What if it was so much bigger
than giving yourself false hope? Find the real
hope, it is out there.

—Josée Leclair

2. THE FOG
AND FINDING YOUR
FOOTING

Melody

THE FOG BEGAN THE MOMENT LIGHTNING STRUCK.

Fog is an unwelcome companion to crisis. It arises like wildfire and dissipates like a slow-blooming desert flower. The fog is disorienting, suffocating. It makes every step and every breath hard to navigate. It ignites a natural survival instinct inside you, but not much more. It's a pace-setter that operates in slow motion.

The fog is unnamed grief and necessary denial, propelling you forward, compelling you to look beyond reality and search for steady footing—only its pathway is dark. There are no obvious trail markers along this path and all you feel is a longing for something, anything, other than what is.

At the time of crisis, your only rumination is "This cannot be happening."

After acting on Luke's request for help and calling my husband at 5:30 a.m. to get his sorry self home from a business trip in Montreal, I slipped into oblivion. I called no one. I sat sorrowfully in denial. Who would believe that this was happening to Luke, to Serge, me, and our family—again, four years after having already lived this hell with our eldest child?

It must be a nightmare, I thought. *I'm going to wake up, and this will not be true.*

Anger rose within me. I resented the thought that Luke would struggle with mental illness, too. Wasn't one child enough? What had I missed? Was there something I should have learned the first time to avoid finding myself here again? Was this some kind of cruel punishment? Where was the escape button?

These questions plagued me. If only I could disappear, take a one-way flight to anywhere but here.

My husband was much harder to read. He immediately jumped into crisis mode and began to act, distract, and play it cool. No emotions, just action. Serge continued to work as best he could and appeared to take things one day at a time, while my future fell apart. My work, accomplishments, dreams, and aspirations seemed meaningless and disengaged from my reality. I felt robbed of the life I knew, and empty to respond. I couldn't give what I didn't have.

Yet somehow I managed to keep putting one foot in front of the other. I attribute this more to the faithful prayers of my fellow believers than strength of my own accord.

I cried and felt sorry for myself, and our child, daily. I was embarrassed by our circumstance and reluctant to ask or accept support from our friends and community in the same "needy" manner for a second time. How humiliating, how humbling. What would others think? Would they question our reality, Luke's diagnosis, our ability to cope? Would they think we were just making this up for the attention? Who knew what others really thought, but my shadow side sure did a good job of trying to guess.

Added to all this was my heartache over our daughters' shock and horror. Karina, our middle child and the only one not to be diagnosed with bipolar disorder, had been so compassionate up to this point but now became calloused. Josée, our eldest, was numb from the realization that what was happening to Luke had happened to her just four years prior. Imagine the bravery she had to muster just to visit him in the hospital, a place where she had resided during some of the worst periods of her life. Adding insult to injury was seeing the same staff who had cared for Josée now caring for Luke. It came as a double-edged sword; the familiarity was helpful, but the pitying looks we received were not.

Thankfully, the girls were too young to visit Luke on the unit, which likely curtailed potential triggers for Josée. We solicited social work support and booked regular meeting times for the girls to vent, cast doubt, ask questions, and grieve. Josée remained very stoic, while Karina began to crack, underlining the fact that this was all too much for one person or family to bear. Fatigue overtook her body and mind. With encouragement from Serge and me, as well as her social worker, Karina reluctantly approached her school for emotional support and academic accommodation. It was especially difficult for Karina to adjust and slow down to the rhythm of her bodily state—the impact of grief, no doubt—because keeping busy was a means of survival.

The Eyes of the Water

The reflection is telling, looking back at you
through the mirror waters are those fiery eyes,
blinking you a pep talk, you're really seeing
yourself flipped and that's all you really know,
and what others vocalize to you of course, you
dip your fingers in the sound waters, and swirl
your face in circles, you are tempted to fall
through the eyes of the lake, what difference
would that make you thought, you jump in fully
clothed, feeling the cold springs linger on the
surface of your skin, your overwhelming tears
seemingly raise the level of the lake, maybe you
found precisely what you're looking for, how did
the waters know you just needed to be embraced
to let you know it's ok, there's a place to add
company to other fallen tears.

—Josée Leclair

3. COMEDY
OF
ERRORS

Melody

As if this weren't enough, quite a sequence of events took place within a short period. Around the time of Luke's crisis, Karina's best friend invited her to go to Disney World for March break as a means of getting away from our family chaos. Karina looked forward to it; she packed, counted down the days, and awaited this magical experience. Four days before the trip, Karina's friend's father died of a massive heart attack, changing the course of everyone's lives.

Obviously the trip was cancelled, and grief abounded. The same evening we received word that her friend's father had passed, Karina and I went together to support the family. I found myself ill-equipped to stand amidst someone else's crisis when I was very much in the depths of my own. It was both selfish and loving to acknowledge my limits, and then remove myself from their home within an hour of arriving. By the time Karina and I quietly slipped away, the family was surrounded by friends and family who were able to uphold them in their time of need.

Although it may seem inappropriate to joke about a situation such as this, humour became a necessary tool to help us through. Josée, with great wisdom, concluded early on in the crisis that it wouldn't be a good choice for her to remain in Headwaters, an experiential outdoors program that takes students outside the school walls. While away, her in-school supports were out of reach. So just weeks into the program, she opted to return to the mainstream. As the second semester was already in motion, she took whatever courses she could get.

As the stress mounted, it wasn't long before her four-course load turned into two. Her plan to graduate within the year and start college in the fall seemed less and less likely given the realities of maintaining optimal health amidst her many stressors. However, her determination kicked in. She eventually found her stride and obtained all four of her credits. She also wrote an aptitude test for admittance to college after taking a campus tour and setting her head and heart on the program of her choice.

Did I mention that she was also falling head over heels in love with her first boyfriend? The day she planned to admit her love for him, everything came crashing down. Long story short, he broke up with her and she simultaneously discovered that she'd been turned down by the college. Talk about heartbreak.

There were days when so many of our family members were crying about something that I called my parents to come and just sit with us for comfort while I tried to disappear into the abyss. Unfortunately, the darkness just grew deeper.

Fire-Lit Eyes

Wind stunned by a truck, waiting to cross, car
after car, over your shoulder checking, when you
look to the left, the wind makes itself known
against your skin, you spot movement out of the
corner of your eye, swoosh, a truck whips by,
leaving your hair in knots, your skin prickling
with goosebumps, you are stunned, leaving a
feeling of invigoration adding fire to your eyes.

—Josée Leclair

4. WHEN THINGS SMOULDER

Melody

WHERE THERE IS A SPARK, THERE'S FIRE.

During this same timeframe, unbeknownst to my sister Val and her husband Rick, a recalled dehumidifier in their basement began to smoulder. It continued for days, leaving no trace other than unwelcome fumes that smelled like burning plastic. Eventually the smouldering escalated into a chemical fire that displaced them from their home indefinitely. They left with only one week's worth of clothing and no idea when they could return. In one moment, everything had changed.

Boy, could I relate. My sister and brother-in-law found themselves living out of suitcases in a local hotel room with two teens, the boyfriend of one of their daughters, and two dogs. That's a lot of upheaval. Insurance agents took over their homestead and began peeling back the layers of smoke damage that had been brewing beneath the house's interior. Piece by piece their house was dismantled and essentially reconstructed. No belonging was left untouched. Every single item had to be inspected and either set aside to be sterilized or pitched.

I cannot imagine how I would process a crisis like theirs. Of course, the irony is that people were likely thinking the same about us.

I'm reminded that diamonds are made with pressure. We cannot truly know how we would feel or respond to a crisis until it happens to us.

At one point, I asked Val how she was processing the event. She said, "Well. For the most part." She then shared the upside of the house fire: a badly needed tune-up of her piano, and carpet and furniture replacements that were long overdue. Somehow we laughed.

I share this to offer perspective and appreciation for what is truly essential in life. Val and Rick may never be fully compensated for what happened to them, and they may never replace all the artefacts in their home, but their love for one another remains intact. I can relate to that. Although I didn't lose material possessions, or a loved one, I lost the dream of the life I had envisioned for me and my family.

Through the Branches

A forested nightfall, the branches cover the sky,
intertwining haunted shapes, outstretching like
hands, your steps start to pick up as you peer into
the depths of trunks, visualizing a figure made
from the anatomy of the forest, on the hunt for
blood, appearing more and more real, the more it
is enhanced by the darkness, it gives it character,
but still unknown, you can make it known.

—Josée Leclair

HOW TO
5. WITNESS
YOUR CHILD LOSING
HIS MIND
WITHOUT LOSING
YOURS

Melody

EIGHT DAYS INTO TREATMENT AT CAIP, A PSYCH WARD FOR KIDS, Luke was worse off than the day he'd been admitted. To put this in perspective, when Josée had gone into crisis at the same age, at the onset of puberty, she had been hospitalized, diagnosed, treated, and discharged within eight days. So you can well imagine the panic we felt.

Finding an individualized medication combination for Luke proved difficult. The doctors took desperate action and prescribed yet another drug on top of the already considerable number of drugs Luke was taking, which was a lot for a boy his size. At the time, this new medication was considered a "big gun" among antipsychotics. Although it wasn't a desirable drug, and had numerous recognized side effects, prescribing it is the standard of care, in low doses, in cases of severe agitation and behavioural dyscontrol when the health and safety of the patient or others may be compromised if they don't receive it. A number of antipsychotic medications are indicated for this use. In emergency situations, medication choices such as this one are guided by a physician's preference and comfort level, hospital policy, and hospital formulary (what is in stock), among other factors such as what other medications have been tried or are being used regularly by the patient.

Of course, every medication has its benefits and risks. For Luke, the new drug had severe side effects, including a stiff jaw, numb lips, excessive drooling, and rigid motor movements. He was later deemed to be allergic to it. On top of everything else, he was walking like a seventy-year-old man with Parkinson's. That was very tough to see.

These were dark and difficult days for all the members of our family. Luke recalls being so heavily sedated at one point that he actually fell asleep while eating his supper. When he awoke, not realizing it was the next day, he picked up his spoiled milk and drank it. He joked that it was perhaps the hospital's version of cottage cheese. Out of necessity, we all found the humour in the horror.

Luke continued to be paranoid and delusional. He believed the nurses were stealing his socks and cutting holes in them. To side with Luke rather than contradict him, Serge agreed and said, "Yes, why look, there is a hole in every sock"—and he proceeded to stick his hand in every sock's natural opening. As we laughed, I leaned against Luke's pillow, only to discover that it was chock full of miscellaneous socks. I asked Luke what that was about. He said, "Mom, to get the nurses back, I'm hiding my socks on them."

During this period, Serge and I needed to ready ourselves and our girls for each and every visit by calling the charge nurse ahead of time and getting a report on Luke's mood. This allowed us to psychologically prepare ourselves for what we might encounter, as well as plan how short or long the visit might be and what we would do with our time together. For example, a bad day meant a short visit by Luke's bedside, avoiding certain topics, or a visit in the courtyard while tossing around a basketball. On a good day we could get him an in-hospital pass and go to Tim Hortons—or, better yet, a community or home pass for several hours, and sometimes even an overnight.

These choices largely depended where Luke was at in the CAIP unit's privilege pass system. Due to the fact that all the patients were struggling with some form of mental illness, each patient's tolerances to stimuli and stress had to be carefully monitored. The last thing anyone involved wanted was to overwhelm a vulnerable patient or cause a setback in their treatment. Therefore, privileges were built on trust and small steps. After each visit, the nursing staff completed and reviewed a patient and parent evaluation form. The better mood management the patient displayed, the quicker he or she could move through the ranks.

Luke was in isolation for the majority of his stay at CAIP, although he doesn't recall much of it. For the most part, he remained contentedly oblivious to his circumstances.

From our perspective, the nursing staff at CAIP are saints. I cannot imagine doing their job with nearly the compassion and patience most of them have. Of course, the three degrees of separation helps—after all, these are not their children—and they can trade off shifts and patients' states change in the interim.

Serge and I practically earned sainthood as well, for having lived with our circumstances as long as we did without turning on one another, or giving up on ourselves or our family members. Diagnosis and treatment take time, and much to our chagrin we learned that sometimes you have to sit on a hunch until the teacher of experience arrives.

Calling Luke's charge nurse prior to visitations allowed us to prep ourselves and the girls for what we might encounter and observe, making Luke's erratic states more bearable, but it also helped us to know how to act. It was easier for us to know what role we would be called upon to perform. Most day's visits felt more like being part of an improv team!

We also knew that the nursing staff, social worker, and sometimes the doctor were available to answer our questions and provide debriefing support as necessary. During this time, Serge and I relied heavily on each other, holding each other up and keeping the other from losing heart. We quickly learned that the middle of a crisis isn't the time to evaluate the status of one's relationship. Our MO was to park our differences and forge ahead. At this stage, we had to use all our available energy to simply endure.

For us, not losing our minds while witnessing our child temporarily losing his meant that we had to go with the flow and try not to overthink things. We had to resist fighting against the realities of our situation. In many cases, our thoughts and emotions followed naturally. We had to allow for tears and venting as required, yet focus as best we could on the care and maintenance of our child, ourselves, and getting through one day—sometimes a single moment—at a time.

Mirror on the Wall

Have you ever looked yourself in the mirror and
not recognised who you are? And wondered
what others even see in you? Have you ever
sat there for so long that you can't help but let
tears slide down your cheeks? Because you feel
as though you don't know who you are. But
if you look long enough, you see something
different. A spark that's lit in your eye that tells
you, there is no one who thinks exactly the way
you do. Your thoughts are unlike anyone else's.
So why conform? Why be like the person next
to you, when you can offer something different
to someone else's horizon? What is seen in you
is something different and that's what attracts
them. This is who you are, and A, B and C
makes you authentically you. The mirror doesn't
show you every part of you, just what's on the
outside. The rest is brought out by those around
you. Give looking in the mirror a new meaning.

—Josée Leclair

6. REWIND

Melody

IF WE ARE REALLY HONEST WITH OURSELVES WHEN WE LOOK BACK, we long suspected Luke's diagnosis. For years, Luke struggled with emotional regulation, often resulting in fits of anger. He suffered from low self-esteem and found friendships to be a challenge. He was always rigid on rules in sports, and in life, and was maladaptive to any kind of change. He ruminated on negative thoughts and perseverated on topics of interest for long periods of time.

Luke often misinterpreted life events, which resulted in conflict with peers and family alike. Near the end of Grade Eight, after numerous accounts of being bullied, Luke, in desperation, vocalized that he wanted to die. Since a teacher was within earshot, it was the duty of the principal to report what Luke had said. He encouraged Serge and I to take Luke to the walk-in at the Canadian Mental Health Association (CMHA) for an assessment. From that point on, Luke began to see Josée's psychiatrist, Dr. Edwards. He had been seeing Dr. Edwards for a year and a half prior to his crisis. In fact, he had even begun trialling a medication to try and prevent bipolar mania from emerging.

Our logic in taking these measures had been that we didn't think we could live through another crisis with a child. Famous last words! However, Luke's ego eventually got in the way of our plan. He began resisting treatment and balking at our attempts to help. Due to the lack of similarities between Luke's and Josée's symptoms, we thought we might be trying to fight the wrong diagnosis. With Josée, we had witnessed overt periods of ups and downs, and with Luke it was everything described above, and symptoms of a more aggressive, cyclical nature.

Guilt and second-guessing eventually wore us down, and we agreed to allow Luke to decrease his medication under the supervision of his psychiatrist. Little did we know that this small amount of medication had been holding the dam that was about to break. Coincidently or not, the mania hit within three days of his medication reduction.

During the buildup, we witnessed a shift in mood. He displayed mixed states of irritability, arrogance, agitation, hyperactivity, scattered thinking, and narrated thoughts. He kept coming to "realizations" and shared "aha moments" about life. He declared many solutions to all of life's problems. Luke presented as fast-paced, with pressured speech, informing people that they may not be able to process everything he had to say. He kept talking to himself, over-empathizing with others while experiencing erratic waves of emotions.

Josée

My brother had been acting stranger than normal. It was as if he was wired, firing out comebacks without stopping the pace of his own mojo. I wasn't thrilled when my parents went to a dinner party one evening and left me alone with him. As soon as I heard the last of my parents' trailing footsteps, I snatched the TV remote, planning to keep myself distracted from Luke's antics.

I soon discovered the plan wasn't well thought out. Luke wanted the basement, and I explained that I wanted the basement TV. He accused me of always getting what I wanted. To avoid what I thought was just a petty fight, I agreed to use the upstairs TV instead. Within seconds of turning it on, he was back. Back and on a mission. Sitting across from me, he accused me of always manipulating him. He claimed that I didn't love him. He said that I had always hated him, that I never even tried to get along with him. It began to get heated. He threw accusations like rapid fire. I couldn't even fight back as he became more amped up and distraught.

At one point, he was no longer sitting; he stood, looked over me, and pointing at me as if I were a child. He thrust his finger at me and kept reminding me that I didn't love him.

I was no longer sure how to calm him down. He started to pace while adding afterthoughts and narrating himself by saying things like "For dramatic emphasis..." after which he'd spit an expletive at me.

In hopes of finding sanctuary, I retreated to my bedroom where I curled up in bed and pulled my knees to my chest. I looked around at the familiar surroundings. I was scared. None of this made sense. I couldn't reconcile with him. Why did he have it in his head that I hadn't ever loved him? Sure, we didn't get along, but I'd like to think I had made some effort.

In the meantime, he still spouted out swears even though had didn't have an audience. I heard him stomp up the stairs. All I could think was, *Oh no, I'm not even safe in my own room.* I decided it would be best to stay meek and quiet until he ran out of fuel. Luke ranted off, returning to his main points. He'd turn to leave. Then, just when I thought he was done, he came back even angrier.

In the short time that he stepped out, I quickly texted Dad. It wasn't uncommon for Luke to lose his temper, so my dad wasn't overly concerned. He just told me to keep my space and they'd return soon.

But this was different; I couldn't even get him to simmer. I didn't have enough time between Luke's visits to convey to my dad the seriousness of what was happening. Luke left one more time, and I risked texting my boyfriend, as any teenager would. He suggested that I lock my room door, which I had forgotten I could do.

I walked across my carpet and slid the lock.

Melody

I recall the evening prior to Luke's fully manic state and hospitalization. He was carrying on as he had the night we'd left him and Josée alone, and with such intensity. Serge was away on business, and the girls and I were at a loss as to how to respond.

I motioned for the girls to stop engaging Luke and come upstairs. There we huddled in Karina's bedroom for refuge. We vented about his unusual behaviour and maddening verbal assaults and actions. Although he posed no obvious threat, we were afraid of his unpredictability. We opted to remain together until he eventually lost steam, even if just momentarily. Soon he would go downstairs to his bedroom.

Somehow there was comfort in numbers, and waiting until the storm passed seemed like the only plausible choice. We eventually hugged and said goodnight, hoping sleep would benefit us all.

Little did I know what was to come.

Karina

The days leading up to Luke's diagnosis and hospitalization are a bit of a blur. I just remember him being out of sorts, saying things that didn't make sense and having more energy than normal. Luke was irritable, although it seemed as though he could turn his moods on and off. When he was with his friends he was happy-go-lucky, and when he was home he was a jerk. Even mental illness isn't an excuse for being a jerk.

Although he was most often at the home of one of his friends, the times when he was home felt long and miserable because he took up so much space and demanded everyone's attention.

On the morning he woke up the household yelling that he had been struck by lightning, I didn't really think that much of it. I mean, I wasn't surprised by the fact that he was being taken to the hospital. That just meant that someone was going to assess him and get him help. I went to school as per usual and went through the motions, although I don't recall much of the day.

The Heart

It is a funny thing, it is an organ that pumps
blood throughout the body according to biology
but in the eyes of society, it is where the feeling
of love is located. It takes you on a journey of
the heart and you hear lines to go with society's
beliefs like: follow your heart, funny huh?
Science says one thing; the world says another.
What is one thing in common, you ask? It was
all said by humans.

—Josée Leclair

7. NO TWO DIAGNOSES ARE THE SAME

Melody

THE DAY OF LUKE'S DIAGNOSIS WAS THE SAME DAY SERGE AND I became elite members of a club nobody wants to be a part of. We weren't just parents of one child with bipolar disorder, but two. I remember the overwhelming sense of just how impossible this situation was. I truly couldn't get past the recurring vision of mountain peaks so tall that their heights could never be reached. This was our Mount Everest, only we had very little preparation or equipment to enable us to make the climb.

For me, there was no comfort in having traversed this course once before, nor any reassurance in knowing this was uncommon, so uncommon that none of the three psychiatrists involved had any prior experience working with families like ours.

Statistics reveal that one percent of the general population has been diagnosed with bipolar disorder. Children with a parent or sibling who has it are four to six times more likely to develop the illness.[2] What makes our situation so unique is that the percentage of people with early-onset bipolar disorder is far lower than the majority of people who get diagnosed later in life.

This is why the chances of having two adolescent siblings with early-onset bipolar disorder are drastically reduced, which explains why

---

2   Candida Fink, MD, "Bipolar Disorder & Heredity—The Genetic Link: Part I," *PsychCentral.* July 24, 2008 (https://blogs.psychcentral.com/bipolar/2008/07/bipolar-disorder-heredity-%E2%80%93-the-genetic-link-part-i/).

there are very few documented cases. The odds of having siblings diagnosed with early-onset bipolar disorder is comparable to being struck by lightning twice—an especially poignant metaphor, given that Luke's first episode revolved around him experiencing a lightning strike.

Our children's experiences with diagnosis and treatment were so divergent that perhaps it shouldn't have been surprising that my husband's and my reactions to the grief was so different as well. In a manic state, Josée was like a happy drunk, seeing and hearing angels and fairies and thinking Selena Gomez was coming for tea. Luke experienced mania as an angry drunk, paranoid, delusional, and in your face with finger-wagging and blaming others for his perceived appraisals of situations. He was difficult to be around.

For me, grief came like a thief in the night, hijacking my rational thoughts and skewing all my emotions. It was insidious, permeating every dimension of life. Grief compelled me to explore and re-evaluate all my thoughts, values, and beliefs, and to question life and faith. It left me feeling exhausted, depleted, and in need of serious self-care and external support.

For my husband, grief approached like a cool, collected cat. It may have clawed at his heart strings, but with little to no apparent hold. Serge seemed to grieve with his hands. The busier he was, the better. As long as he had a cell phone, power tool, or blueprint to occupy his hands and mind, he was content.

I call this "man's play therapy." So long as we wives don't judge it, the actions of our husbands may serve a greater purpose. This, to Serge, is downtime. Time to think, time to process, and time to heal… or is it to escape? Only he can say. We all have to find ways to cope and heal in healthy ways. For Serge, it may involve a renovation. For me, it may include a shopping spree or day at the spa—or both! I have come to understand that my spouse is not a measuring stick of my healing.

When Josée was diagnosed, it came as a welcome answer and solution, explaining her behaviour and states. When Luke was diagnosed, we received it as an unwelcome life sentence for which none of us was prepared. It felt so unfair, as if mental illness should be inflicting itself upon some other unsuspecting, inexperienced family, not ours.

While in treatment, Luke, true to his character, coveted the hospital rules and adhered to them as though his life depended on it. Josée had tried to trick the system and fool the psychiatrist by downplaying her symptoms and requesting an early discharge, which was contrary to her character. It's funny how their unique temperaments emerged in mania; sometimes they stayed true to character and other times not at all.

I cannot explain the pain of seeing your child look like themselves, but not act like themselves. If I took the time to overthink this, I might wonder which version was the truer one. That's one of the frustrations of the disorder. Mania can be experienced as an unfiltered version of you. As parents, the grief associated with this paradox is akin to witnessing a living death. It's the experience of observing the separation of a body and a mind, as though the essence of your child was temporarily displaced and you were merely left with his or her physical form.

Perhaps it was a situation such as this that inspired the expression "strangely familiar." Regardless, the phrase fits. It's witnessing a presence of body, but not of mind, much like watching a loved one go through a form of dementia.

Did Josée's experience with mental illness, though different, still prepare us in many ways for Luke's? Yes. It came as a hidden gem, or a paradox. I learned in grad school that things are not always either/or, but often both/and. As a friend, Collin, once said, "The good news is you have been through this before. The bad news is you have been through this before."

We knew all too well what had taken place with Luke and what was yet to come. That made it especially difficult to take things one day at a time. How could I not get ahead of myself? One thing was for sure: I knew that I didn't have the capacity to do it all again. How would we give Luke what he needed, and do it differently than we had with Josée? A righteous anger rose within me as a call to change: "I cannot do this!"

Having acknowledged that truth, we gently shoved Josée back into counselling, and lovingly suggested that if she wanted independence, she would need to grow it. Serge and I couldn't be endlessly available to her for all her emotional and practical needs. We needed to see signs of readiness, and willingness, to do the necessary work to grow up and manage her illness in order to be college-ready the following September.

Serge and I also made a commitment to streamline our supports and have the whole family see one therapist. Community supports are great, but we wanted them to think of treating the whole family instead of just a single patient, particularly since that patient was a child. What we wouldn't have done to have the psychiatrist, family doctor, therapists, and blood work lab all in the same facility.

Just Listening

Her eyes turned to peeks of wonder, something
was brewing behind those eyes. I sat there at
the café table, as enchantment struck her mind,
the music whispered into her ear, enticing her
thoughts to dance through scenes she made
up long ago, matching her facial expressions to
her changing thoughts. She'd used the setting
around her to shape her imagination. I stared at
her, watching her eyes through the candle lit fire;
you could almost see her play with the sequences
that made up her being. Each song brought her a
new feel to the experience; I'm reminded of what
brings me joy.

—Josée Leclair

8. HUMOUR IN THE HEARTBREAK

Melody

"The world's record for most times getting hit by lightning and surviving is seven," said comedian Harrison Greenbaum on an episode of *America's Got Talent*. "What an emotional journey. The first time you get hit by lightning, you're probably, like, surprised. The second time you get hit, you're like, what are the odds? The third or fourth time, you're just, like, this is who I am. By the fifth time… why am I so bad at outside? By the sixth or seventh time… I think I have a superpower, but I have no idea how to use it."[3]

Just as in Greenbaum's example, our family had to find humour in the heartbreak. In both of our stories, lightning was thematic.

A necessary skill in order to watch your kids lose their minds without losing yours is to find humour in the heartbreak.

Instead of disagreeing with your child's interpretation of reality, at times you have to play along to avoid escalating the situation. On one particular hospital visit with Luke, the rest of the family was a little apprehensive, wondering what state we would find him in. That day, at first glance, he appeared normal, or back to his baseline. We all sighed with relief that our "Lukey boy" was coming back.

As it turned out, the longer our visit lasted, the more obvious it became that we couldn't have been more wrong. We were playing cards in a

---

3   Harrison Greenbaum on *America's Got Talent*, "Auditions Week Six," July 11, 2017.

booth in the hospital lounge, engaging Luke in small talk. We asked him how he passed the time. Luke told us that he had limited interaction with the other patients, and therefore spent a lot of time alone in his room. He went on to say that he amused himself by playing tic-tac-toe.

We wondered how that worked.

"Well, I win a lot," Luke said.

I set a card on the pile in the middle of the table. "Do you play hang man?"

Luke looked a little horrified. "Hang man is a 'trigger' word on the ward, Mom. The inpatients call the game snowman."

"Ah. That makes sense."

Luke played a card and then, out of the blue said, "Don't you think it's weird I don't have any scars from being hit by lightning?"

I had just taken a sip of my coffee and was so taken aback that I nearly spewed it all over the table. The girls winced and rolled their eyes. Luke didn't see them, but I could read their thoughts loud and clear: *Oh no, not this script again.*

Serge tried to recover the situation. "What does that lead you to conclude, son?"

Luke shrugged. "I guess I'm just lucky."

We quickly changed the subject.

There were also the times when Luke would put his disjointed thoughts on paper and try to piece them together, coming to a kind of satisfying meaning that was gibberish to us. We would all nod our heads in approval, smiling and saying "Aha" while trying to hold back laughter.

Josée especially found it difficult not to laugh in his face. She wanted to shout "You don't make any sense" while the rest of us stayed in character. As far as we were concerned, it was worth the effort to keep the peace and uphold the façade that Luke was doing as mentally well as he thought he was. Certainly there had been some incremental improvement.

At one point in Luke's manic/delusional state, he thought that he was under 24/7 observation. He was sure the nurses were intentionally setting him up in order to catch him doing something he wasn't supposed to do. He was tormented by these thoughts, and it broke our hearts to see him so beside himself and out of his right mind.

The brain is a powerful organism. It's as though the glass ceiling in Luke's mind had been removed and there was no limit to the thoughts or actions he could conjure up. Luke talked about this as a matter of fact. He seemed to have lost any kind of filter on his thoughts.

During Luke's manic state, he was very impulsive. He would contradict himself, announcing one thing and then doing the opposite. One time he came home for a visit, and just before his friends arrived he announced, "Now, we're not going to talk about my situation or why I'm in the hospital." We all agreed, but the minute his friends arrived he began to spill the beans himself. I lovingly redirected him and realized that this would need to be a supervised visit. His friends were really good about it. They very much picked up from where they had last left off and began laughing, joking, and carrying on, just the way it should be.

Karina, Luke, Nico, Kyle, and Ellie, playing it cool.

Lost Voice

speaking through a webbed throat, caught
behind fear, tucked away in made up walls,
where the words are intentionally safe, bleeding
into the thought of false thinking that your voice
isn't valid, wearing yesterday's hurt of unsaid
thoughts, winged into the fog, planted into the
thinking it's unreasonable, raising unspoken
thoughts, my voice feels purposeless, drowned
out by the noise, I fear it's better to not say
anything at all than to say something you regret,
leaving empty breath and pin drop silences, I'm
on the line if I don't speak soon, it's all described
by a silenced fragment, say the first word, it's
step one. The rest will follow.

—Josée Leclair

9. TREATMENT CONTINUED

Melody

AFTER TWENTY-ONE DAYS OF TREATMENT AT CAIP, LUKE WAS STILL struggling with racing thoughts and coming in and out of manic states. No one knew for sure whether or not his pre-existing condition, ADHD, and the treatment he had received for it was playing a role in his slow recovery. His ADHD medication was a stimulant, and Luke's medical team speculated that there was a chance it was interfering with the effectiveness of the antipsychotic medication. In fact, in rare circumstances the combination could possibly trigger another manic episode.

After much deliberation, the doctor discontinued his ADHD medication. Within days, the antipsychotics proved effective. Now the challenge became whether or not to reintroduce the original medication. Was Luke's diagnosis of ADHD legitimate, or had he merely had bipolar disorder all along? Or perhaps he had concurrent disorders?

"It is suspected that a significant number of children diagnosed in the United States with attention-deficit disorder with hyperactivity (ADHD) actually have early-onset bipolar disorder instead of or alongside of ADHD."[4] This makes arriving at an accurate diagnosis very tenuous. In fact, there is a significant comorbidity between bipolar disorder and ADHD. Up to twenty-four percent of adults with bipolar disorder

---

4   Rashmi Nemade and Mark Dombeck, "Statistics and Patterns in Bipolar Disorder," *MentalHelp.net*. August 7, 2009 (https://www.mentalhelp.net/articles/statistics-and-patterns-in-bipolar-disorder/).

can also have ADHD. A significant challenge is that ADHD presents itself much earlier in life than the cardinal symptoms of bipolar disorder, meaning that individuals will likely be treated for ADHD before bipolar disorder fully declares itself.

That's what happened with Luke. At this point, changing his meds was like playing Russian roulette, and nobody wanted to take that chance. The tension built at CAIP, as the staff felt the pressure to help Luke get better or refer him to another facility. After all, they specialized in acute care. Thankfully, because I'm a counsellor, I was able to use my therapeutic knowledge of supports and suggested Parkwood Institute for longer-term specialized care.

The staff agreed that he may be a good candidate for Parkwood. However, the social worker warned us of Parkwood's selective patient process. We were told that his referral could take three to four days to process. Then, if he was selected, it could be another two to three weeks for Luke to be transferred, pending bed availability. Serge and I said we would take our chances, motivated by Luke's need for ongoing care and our full recognition of how tenuous it could be to have him return home and potentially upset Josée's mood stability.

Within twenty-four hours, our prayers were answered. Not only did Parkwood accept him, they were able to admit him within days.

Unfortunately, the communication between us and the hospitals was murky at best. Firstly, it was a CAIP nurse who informed us of Luke's acceptance to Parkwood, rather than his psychiatrist. To make matters worse, she announced it casually to Serge and I right in front of Luke, who had no idea that this was part of a larger plan. Secondly, when I called Parkwood on the day of the transfer to ask what our role and responsibilities were in the process, I was informed by an operator that standard practice was for Serge and I to be at the hospital upon Luke's arrival at 10:00 a.m. Considering we had a two-hour drive ahead of us and it was already 8:00 a.m., I barely said goodbye before Serge and I dropped everything to go. We made it just in the nick of time.

I recall walking into the Parkwood Institute, finding the adolescent ward, and discovering Luke already there, patiently waiting. He seemed so docile, calm, and unfazed by the transfer, a clear sign to us that he still wasn't himself; Luke typically doesn't adjust well or quickly to any sort of change. Even the social worker documented Luke's unusual cooperation for a teen his age in her case notes. Serge and I chuckled at this.

"This is such an upgrade from the basement ward at CAIP," Luke remarked.

We were then introduced to Luke's new medical team. There began the lengthy, and now quite annoying, process of retelling Luke's history, only this time it was up to Luke. His recollections and insights were cloudy, to say the least.

After Luke was dismissed from the meeting, Serge and I shared from our perspective where Luke was at and our continued concerns and hopes for his treatment. I specifically remember telling the staff not to be fooled by his intellect, charm, and self-proclaimed insight. Although these are some of Luke's natural qualities, they might lead him to present a heightened version of himself. Anything he said in his manic state needed to be accepted with caution.

Once Luke was settled in, Serge and I left with an optimistic assurance that Luke was in the right place and would be well cared for. We told each other that it was our job now to look after ourselves, but neither of us knew how we would do that when we had two other children to care for, one of whom also struggled with bipolar disorder.

Still, it was a nice thought—and a small comfort—as we left the hospital, and our son, and headed home.

Knotted

Tied to the thought, grounded in its roots, in roots of reason, one beginning to look smudged, though a perfectly imperfect reason, intertwined and interlocked unthreading creating friction, all to define its intricacy, I remember your voice, it was soaked in sarcasm defining the sound of life. It was uninvited.

—Josée Leclair

10. HOME
VISIT

Melody

IT WASN'T UNTIL WEEKS INTO RECOVERY THAT LUKE EARNED THE privilege of home passes. Even then, he continued to toy with the idea of what was real and what wasn't in his manic state.

One day, I noticed that he kept looking out the living room window. "What's so interesting out there, Luke?" I asked.

He nodded at the window. "Huh. Look at the hydro pole."

Treading lightly, I asked, "What about it?"

"Looks like it isn't broken after all, but how can that be?"

I rested a hand on his shoulder. "How can that be?"

Luke was beginning to see that what he had believed to be facts might actually have been tricks of the mind. We remained in each other's company, soaking in the silence of Luke's newfound revelation.

The truth was sinking in, and so was the grief that came from understanding that what he had believed to be true might not be true at all. Inconceivable.

To Miss Is Rather Beautiful

It means it meant something to you, things you
didn't even realize you remembered come into
play when you miss something, without noticing
you gave the memory substance, it stained you,
it will come in waves at any given moment.
Something gravitates the memory, fading into
the setting, glossing tears over your eyes. You
remember.

—Josée Leclair

11. AN OASIS IN THE DESERT

Melody

THE OXFORD DICTIONARY'S DEFINITION OF OASIS IS "A FERTILE SPOT in a desert, where water is found… a pleasant or peaceful area or period in the midst of a difficult or hectic place or situation."[5] As our family found itself in the midst of a difficult and hectic a situation we could never have imagined, we needed an oasis more than ever before.

It wasn't long before reality set in. Serge and I recognized we could no longer visit Luke ever day due to the distance. Parkwood was more than an hour away.

This decision came with both relief and concern. How would we remain close enough to ensure the quality care of our priceless possession? A friend of mine referred us to The Ronald McDonald House, which we knew very little about. It provides a place for the families to stay while their children are in hospital. It did sound like a possible solution for us, though, so we had Luke's social worker make the referral.

We toured the facility and learned about their services. It was an impressive place. From the moment we set foot on the property, we were lavished with love, gifts, and ultimate care and concern. Essentially, we were told that we could come and go as we pleased. We were merely encouraged to keep the staff informed of all registered guests. They assured

---

5   *Oxford Living Dictionaries,* "Oasis." Date of access: August 14, 2018 (https://en.oxforddictionaries.com/definition/oasis).

us that as long as a caregiving member of the family was present at least once in any twenty-four-hour period, the room would remain ours. Talk about a home away from home. It was the closest thing to an all-inclusive resort we were going to get under the circumstances.

It was surreal and humbling to know that every single person who resided at The Ronald McDonald House also had a loved one struggling to maintain his or her health in one way or another. There was an unspoken mutual respect between all residents as families went about their business, caring for the needs of themselves and each other.

One man called out to Serge, remarking, "You're French." This man was from Fort Frances in northwestern Ontario, approximately 1,500 kilometres away, a seventeen-hour drive. He had been in London for months without hearing his mother tongue. It struck me that displaced people seek out the simple comforts, like a familiar language.

The Ronald McDonald House offered room, board, and entertainment. Volunteers from within the community provided one home-cooked meal every day, while the rest of the meals could be self-made in the common kitchen with everyday staples and fresh fruits, vegetables, and dairy products. Each guest was provided with a fridge for additional meals and snacks, or for those with specific nutritional needs. And if that wasn't enough, leftovers from the night before were available to whoever wanted them. Daily baked goods and fresh coffee were also available at the self-servery.

Did I mention we could also fill takeout containers for our loved ones to give them a break from hospital food? This was clearly a highlight for Luke. I will never forget the day he went on and on to the Ronald McDonald House staff about horrible the oven-baked hospital spaghetti had tasted. He kept saying how bad it was and questioning who could cook spaghetti that way. Clearly the hospital food paled in comparison to the meals offered by The Ronald McDonald House.

Apart from the food, there was a workout gym, a games room, a craft room, book nooks, libraries, and a theatre with surround sound, lazy boy recliners, and a popcorn machine. Needless to say, these spaces provided a safe refuge for us and a good place to bring Luke when he was given a hospital pass. It gave us a place to be and things to do in the safety of a sensitive, empathetic environment. It truly was an oasis.

The staff knew us by name, and even though the building physically resembled a hotel, it was so much more. The staff oozed thoughtfulness and compassion. Serge travels for a living, and he had never experienced the balance between independence and service such as we experienced there. We were able to host friends and family and walk around in our pjs at all hours of the day or night without judgment.

During this time, we had a visit from my youngest brother Darryk and his wife Christa along with their three kids, Ella, Sophie, and Caleb. Josée's friend Jack also joined us. My brother went out and bought the makings for subs and he and Serge put them together in the common kitchen. We all sat together to share a family meal. It was such a wonderful taste of normalcy.

The kids proved to be a great distraction for Luke, as he had recently been experiencing anxious distress. It was as though he was afraid of his own shadow, not to mention sharp objects of any sort. Any time we walked through the kitchen to get to the games room, Luke would ask to hold my hand, as though the "sharps" could jump out of the drawers and hurt him, a reminder to me of the power of thought and mind.

Our nieces and nephew expected Luke to be the funny guy they knew him to be, and Luke did not disappoint. However, Karina recalls that at one point during the visit Luke's paranoia and distress set in and he reprimanded her for throwing Caleb in the air and making him laugh too hard. Luke had felt that Karina was being too rough and insisted that Caleb could get hurt. I think Luke's abrupt, explosive reaction scared both Caleb and Karina.

Our parents were also a big support. At one point, my parents relieved us at The Ronald McDonald House so we could attend a wedding. Not long afterwards, Serge's parents came all the way from Elliot Lake and did the same, allowing Serge and I time to catch our breath and process all that was happening.

I don't know what we would have done without the support of friends and family in all forms and on all levels—emotionally, physically, financially, spiritually, and relationally.

After Luke had been at Parkwood for seven days, we found that his anxious distress was heightening—so much so that he became difficult to be around, even for us. He was virtually inconsolable. He required an exhausting amount of reassurance in order to do anything. Serge and I could only last twenty minutes at a time with him before we'd have to switch out. Even the hospital staff was at a loss to know how to manage his symptoms and provide Luke comfort.

After many failed attempts to assist Luke in self-regulating his emotions, they decided to place him on a 24/7 watch, meaning that a staff person was with him constantly for a couple of days. It seemed as though having a constant physical presence was the key to Luke being able to overcome his discomfort, settle in, and manage his distress.

The meds finally appeared to be taking effect as well. All of the combined efforts got him through.

When some family members visited one day, Luke shared with us about his anxiety toolbox, which was full of coping strategies. These included deep breathing techniques, grounding techniques, calm place visualizations, sketching and colouring mandalas, holding weighted objects (in Luke's case, weighted frogs in various sizes), running his fingertips lightly across looped stitched washcloths, naming worry tissues and throwing them in the garbage, listening to music, and going through positive self-talk scripts.

Here is one such script that Luke wrote while in hospital, shared from his journal:

I want to be here until I am better
Things will get better
This is a safe place
They will take care of me
I am loved
Use the anxiety box
Get stronger today
Daily reads
Others' problems are not mine
No one can get in my head unless I let them

I am safe
I can cope
I have strategies
Healthy reads

Although these tools could have been perceived as juvenile, we were grateful for them. To our great relief, they seemed to help him to turn a corner.

After the 24/7 watch came Q-15, Q-30, and Q-60, which are codes for the constant checks on him every fifteen, thirty, or sixty minutes. The length of time between checks got longer until Luke was eventually out of the woods.

As Luke's manic symptoms began to dissipate, he insisted on working out on the treadmill for twenty minutes per day. He was quite emphatic about the rate and pace at which he worked out. We all got roped into his workouts at some point, including Uncle Darryk. We knew Luke was getting better when he no longer believed he had to keep his heart rate up to "be normal."

Remaining in our oasis also took the form of overnight getaways for Serge and me. This is always something we have prioritized, whether in crisis or not. We even snuck away for an overnight at a hotel in the middle of Luke's crisis.

As I write this, we are on one of our escapes. It is so important to carve out this time for ourselves. It's an escape from caregiving, even if only for a short time. It's good for the soul to recharge, just as we do for all of our electronic gadgets. Each time we do this, we demonstrate the inestimable value of upholding the care of ourselves and our partner.

Where Is the Light?

A girl was running, she was running from the
darkness, because that is all she has ever been
taught to do, suddenly someone stopped her in
her tracks and spoke, "What are you running
from?" she responded, "I am running- running
from fear, from past, from hurt." The person told
her to stop, and said, "Walk with me, I will create
your hope."

—Josée Leclair

12. THE IMPORTANCE OF TRADITIONS AND A TRIBE

Melody

FOR THE PAST SIX YEARS, THE GIRLS AND I HAVE PARTICIPATED IN AN annual mother-daughter retreat with our closest friends—our tribe. Steven Handel, in an article about how we've lost our tribal mentality, explains,

> A tribe is a group of people that care for each other and look out for each other no matter what. They are bonded by a strong sense of shared values, meaning, and purpose in life. In most cases, they are even willing to fight and die for each other…
>
> There's an old cliché that nothing brings people together like a common enemy, and there turns out to be a lot of truth to this.[6]

I wasn't particularly feeling up to it this year, after the storm we had weathered over the last three months, but as my girls and their friend Lauren would say, "You don't mess with tradition." Besides, the others would have been very disappointed if we hadn't gone, and I think we had

---

6   Steven Handel, "How We've Lost Our Tribal Mentality—and Why It Hurts Us as a Society," *The Emotion Machine.* August 23, 2016 (http://www.theemotionmachine. com/how-weve-lost-our-tribal-mentality-and-why-it-hurts-us-as-a-society/).

all been through enough disappointment by this point. So we put our feelings aside and went.

Historically, there has always been a lot of fun and laughter over the course of the weekend. As we've aged, us moms have noticed that it's resulted in a lot of piddles in our panties. Note to self for subsequent years: wear panty liners—or better yet, Depends! I'm beginning to wonder if our teens can relate, since they use the buzz term "cuddle puddles." Although to them this phrase means a group hug.

Anyway, we eat, laugh, stay up far too late, and wear pjs most of the weekend—unless, of course, we're forced to go out.

The part of the weekend that never ceases to amaze me is the Sunday morning church service, which the girls lead. Over the years, we've shared testimonies, poetry, worship, communion, scripture readings, and personal reflections. The year Luke was "struck by lightning," the girls did all that and more, ending with plenty of warm fuzzies. What are warm fuzzies? It's a circle time where we take turns sharing what we mean to each other. Not only did we all cry, I'm pretty sure we ended in a cuddle puddle.

There were a lot of meaningful moments on this trip, but the most profound thing to me was my daughter Karina's devotion and personal reflection. If God wasn't holding a megaphone to my ear, I don't know who was.

She read:

"For he will order his angels to protect you wherever you go" (Psalm 91:11, NLT).

The future is like a huge mountain looming in front of you. Its peaks are spiked with troubles, and its sides are pitted with problems. How can you face something so huge?

The real trouble is not the mountain—it's that you're looking only at the mountain. And because you aren't looking at where you're going right now, you stumble on the easy path of today.

I know how much that future mountain worries you. But it may not even be part of your path. You don't know what will happen today, much less tomorrow. I may suddenly turn you away from the mountain, or show you an easier path. But I promise that if I ask you to climb that mountain, I will give you everything you need to reach the top. My angels will protect you. And I will be right by your side every step of the way.

Additional Readings taken from: Psalm 18:29, Psalm 91:12, and 2 Corinthians 5:7.[7]

Karina

It's so simple, but so true. Life is full of ups and downs. Mountains and valleys, waves and still waters, loud yet quiet, peaceful but chaotic, rocky but smooth... yes, life is full of ups and downs. We will never be completely happy. It's impossible to have joy without sadness. We are constantly trying to balance our lives, but the truth is that there will always be a mountain to climb.

We often get caught up in the mountain and how big it is, and how hard the journey may be. We get caught up in all this worry before we even climb. We need to learn how to live by faith and trust, let go of worry, and have faith that we will make it to the top of that mountain!

I love to rock-climb. When I rock-climb, I often get worried. Will I make it to the top of the climbing wall? How will I make the next move? But then I tell myself to live by faith and not by sight. I tell myself, "If God put you to it, he will bring you through it." Then, when I get on the wall, it all just comes to me and before I know it I have completed the problem!

Sometimes we've just got to trust that God's got it all in his hands. I know this is easy to say and that actually doing it can be very difficult. Worry is inevitable. It's like something that's always there. So I'm not saying that you have to stop worrying—because, let's be honest, it's impossible to stop worrying—but at least try to let go and let God, even if it's just buying something for yourself or trusting that you'll do well on that test. Whatever it is, it's a start. We all need to live with a little less worry. We all need to aspire to live by faith and not by sight.

---

7   Sarah Young, *Jesus Calling* (Nashville, TN: Thomas Nelson, 2004), 293. Material taken from *Jesus Calling* by Sarah Young Copyright © 2004 by Sarah Young. Used by permission of Thomas Nelson. www.thomasnelson.com.

Trust in God. Worry ends when faith begins.

Melody

Talk about truth coming out of the mouths of babes. How could Karina have known that she was speaking directly to my heart? Throughout this time of crisis, the most recurring image in my mind was of a mountain, and I had kept thinking the word *Impossible* like a mantra.

What I took from this message is that God gave me more than I can bear, but he didn't give me more than *he* can bear. When we lean on God, his strength is made perfect in weakness.

The Heart's Cry

If only one could hear the sharp whimpers of
the heart, how their choices would change. It is
where the underlying emotions exist. Untouched
because of fear. If only I had heard your heart's
cry—it could have been different. Would it have
been different if you had heard mine? Instead it
is left in unheard echo.

—Josée Leclair

13.

SEEK
AND RECEIVE
PEOPLE
IN YOUR
CORNER

Melody

ONE PARTICULARLY DIFFICULT DAY, SERGE AND I DECIDED TO ASK OUR new pastor, Debra, whether or not she saw walk-ins. She said, "Why, yes." In fact, that very day she had an appointment booked and asked if we could come back in the afternoon.

Serge and I took the opportunity to have lunch together. As we were eating, Josée called from school to tell us she was having a panic attack. We said everything we could to calm her down, but before we knew it she showed up. So much for our lunch date. We informed her that she would have to return to school and face the music.

After she had gone, we visited Pastor Debra. To be honest, I was in so much pain that I don't remember the details of our meeting, only the feeling of being heard and validated. Serge recalls her wise words about hope and hopelessness, and ultimately she acknowledged our place of feeling no hope.

Pastor Debra became an integral part of my healing. She willingly hung in there throughout the tension of what was happening, patiently listening to all my questions. She and the church community coordinated weekly meals during this chaotic time, and for that I am grateful. Friends and family also surrounded us with words of encouragement, prayers, cards, money, and gift cards—all practical acts of service. Not only had my income decreased when I took an EI sick leave, but our expenses increased as we had to spend more money on gas, parking, and food when we visited Luke.

Serge

We had only been attending our new church for a couple months before Luke had his episode. Pastor Debra had already reached out to us to get to know us better as parishioners.

After just a few days of Luke being in the hospital, we figured there might be no better time for her to get to know us than now! I remember going into her office and warning her that we were about to drop a bomb on her. I proceeded to tell her what was currently going on with us, and our family history with Josée.

Her response acknowledged our feeling of hopelessness.

My heart sank. Was she telling me there was no hope? Don't pastors always talk about hope? What I believe she meant is that it's okay for us to feel hopeless in a moment. She went on to say that if she had told us there was hope, and offered us the cliché that everything was going to be okay, she would lose credibility—for we would know that she didn't understand where we were at.

This gave me a sense of relief. I wasn't the only one who felt hopeless in this kind of situation, and it was now the responsibility of the people surrounding me to hold on to hope, as they still had the capacity we didn't have.

Pastor Debra's words encouraged me to continue the prayer chain I had started where I could rely on my friends and family to hold us up.

A Single Moment Stopped in Time

Time freezes, and you can feel your warm heart
beating through your body, you feel alive and at
peace—most people think these moments are
rare—I like to think the contrary. I feel it when I
am walking outside, when I am doing the things
I love—like skating or getting lost into a song.
It is called being in the moment and feeling it.
It can happen anytime if you get in touch with
the feelings of the moment. As I skate the wind
tickles my fingertips while I perfect my glides,
I feel free, I feel as though I am being held by
the hands of the wind, as I turn my feet inwards
to make another twist, I let loose as the turn
unravels, and I do the motions to skate circles
around the rink. The sun is seemingly smiling
at me, the clouds are as white as can be, and the
snow winks at me with each sparkle. I listen
around me, I hear the wind running through the
trees, the sound of skates making contact with
ice, and the calmness of my head. It is moments
like these that make me beam.

—Josée Leclair

14. RESOUNDING MOMENTS

Melody

THROUGHOUT THE DURATION OF LUKE'S STAY IN HOSPITAL, IT WAS standard practise for Serge and I to meet weekly with the assigned social worker. Serge couldn't attend several of our face-to-face meetings due to work and joined us instead by conference call. That was challenging, as there were lots of times when Serge was at a disadvantage as a result of missing tone and body language, two integral parts of communication.

Nonetheless, on one occasion when I was having my rightfully deserved weekly meltdown, Penny, the social worker, asked me how I had coped up until now. Where had I drawn my strength? I thought about it in silence and then said, "God."

Over the phone, we could hear Serge scoff and snicker. Penny asked him what he had heard, and Serge reluctantly replied, "Alcohol?" We all burst out laughing. For some, alcohol can be like a god.

My friend Linda is a good friend and nurse. At the time, she was recovering from a concussion that coincidentally had taken place the same day Luke had suffered his manic episode and ended up in the hospital. She had landed arse over tea kettle that day when she stepped out onto her front porch after an ice storm.

So much of what Linda learned about living with a concussion applied to Luke's bipolar disorder. She told me that every daily activity we engage in either energizes or depletes our batteries. Linda had to learn how to balance and manage her limited resources.

Luke's psychiatrist also told us that, from a brain perspective, recovering from a manic episode is much like recovering from a concussion. It takes careful management of stimulation to allow the brain to heal and fully recover cognitions.

Oddly, another good friend of ours, Amanda, was involved in a car accident around this time that resulted in whiplash. During our time off-work, the three of us met weekly for therapeutic lunches. We affectionately referring to ourselves as the Twisted Sisters, since we were all managing various physical ailments and psychological stressors.

Linda once remarked that she and I were working towards digging ourselves out of the trenches side by side. As she put it, "You don't bring me down like some people would in your circumstances, whining and playing the victim. You still show signs of life and are working towards living life to the full." She said something to the effect that it was amazing I was still standing, let alone actively engaged in humour and healing. I thanked her, somewhat tentatively, as it was a compliment—if a bit of a backhanded one.

The three of us went back and forth, swapping experiences about the process of learning to recognize and accept our capabilities and limitations. We also discussed how they might qualify us for employment insurance or short/long-term disability. At one point, I swept a hand around the table and said, "Look at us. Do we look disabled?" It was a good reminder to us that you don't have to look disabled to be disabled.

Looking back, it's amazing to me how much self-judgment we hold, as well as biases, stereotypes, and beliefs that prevent us from reaching out and getting help. This is especially difficult for those who work in the caregiving profession. We can dish out compassion, but it's much harder to ingest.

I'm so thankful for friends, but I have to admit that at times I questioned whether or not they would want to stick around through our neediness.

In her book *Beautiful Battlefields*, author Bo Stern writes, "Sometimes I worry… that my friends will feel like they're out of encouraging things to say and they'll find new friends on happier journeys. Then I remember who my friends are and what they're made of. End of worry."[8]

---

8   Bo Stern, *Beautiful Battlefields* (Colorado Springs, CO: NavPress, 2013), 163.

You Are the Treasure!

This little pink note
The note read "you are the treasure".
I felt differently.
I must have somehow known I'd need it.
Since I kept it all these years.
It was right in front of me.
I think the same is true in life.
I am a speck in this grand universe.
There is purpose.
The past is in the past, it's what made you, YOU!
What are you waiting for?
I know you can do this.
Look up the sun is peeking, looking for you!
Just open up.

—Josée Leclair

15. FIGHTING THE GIANTS

Melody

WHEN COPING WITH MENTAL ILLNESS, A PERSON MUST CONTEND with many giants. One of the biggest is the "formal systems," as I call them: hospitals, community organizations, and benefits—the kind of supports that aren't really supports when you don't precisely fit their black-and-white checkboxes.

Insurance benefit packages caused us a great deal of frustration. While valuable, they are really only a benefit to you if you and your loved ones are perfectly healthy. We faced enormous challenges just attempting to complete the applications, let alone gain approval for our applications.

As we waited to hear back on the first application we submitted, an underwriter who was reviewing our medical histories called to ask Serge to clarify whether his weight was recorded in kilograms or pounds. The call gave us hope. After filling out pages upon pages of medical details for each family member, this was the only detail they wanted confirmed. Maybe we were getting close to an acceptance.

More days passed before we received a letter in the mail telling us that Luke and Josée's applications had been rejected, while Serge's and mine had been accepted, as we were the healthy ones. They also denied payment for Karina's only medication, to treat acne. How generous. Not. We've learned that unless you have a squeaky-clean bill of health, don't even waste your time trying to collect benefits.

That same afternoon, Serge attempted to complete an online application with another provider. He only got partway through, to page four of nine, before he was alerted that the claim would be denied. Nice. How do you like them apples?

Another challenge we faced was related to our attempt to acquire outpatient services for Luke, which was a nightmare. With Josée, we had been inundated with help and supports. With Luke, not so much. The right hand (the referring hospital) did not seem to be talking to the left hand (outpatient services). Much of the paperwork ended up being done by the high school vice principal rather than the in-hospital social worker, and nothing came to fruition until much later, after many, many follow-up phone calls.

One of the discharge plan-of-care components was that Luke continue with dialectical behaviour therapy (DBT). The following is a copy of an email I needed to send to a certain organization we were attempting to deal with, in order to be heard:

Dear Sir,

My name is Melody Leclair and I have a question and concern about the DBT Program. We have a son who was recently diagnosed with bipolar disorder and was hospitalized and treated for over two months. Luke was discharged from The Parkwood Institute in London just before Easter. As part of his discharge plan, he is to continue with Dialectical Behaviour Therapy. A referral was made by our social worker through the Here 24/7 crisis line prior to Luke's discharge. I followed up with them to ask about the process and they gave me the name of the contact person. I spoke with him and was told that, because our son is not suicidal or self-harming, he would not be eligible to attend as he does not fit the criteria for the group. I should mention at this point that our family has a history with both your organization and the person I spoke with, and was appalled by his response. Our son just came out of crisis, and now he cannot get support unless he is in crisis? Help me understand your process here.

Melody

After yet another follow-up call, Serge and I were invited to attend a meeting with the managers of the organization. Our apprehensions quickly diminished when, early in the conversation, we were offered an apology for the fact that they had seemingly dropped the ball. They explained that their DBT process was in stark contrast to the hospital's DBT process. At Parkwood, DBT was used as a general skills-building tool, covering a wide range of mood disorders and/or behavioural concerns. DBT was reserved for those who were in crisis—self-harming or actively suicidal.

Given that criteria, Luke would not be a fit. But they did offer us other services, both individual and group therapeutic supports.

During this meeting, we also had the opportunity to reflect on Luke's discharge experience and offer constructive criticism to help strengthen in-patient and out-patient transfers. We learned that wording in referrals is everything. Instead of requesting a niche service such as DBT, they advised us that it's best to request services more broadly, using terms such as "individual and suitable group therapy supports." We believe that it would be beneficial if social workers, who take care of these services, were aware of these sorts of recommendations and could pass that information along to others attempting to acquire supports.

The key when working with systems is to be both polite and persistent, although sometimes you just need the latter. It is important to remember that individuals often don't have control over the system, and so they have to learn to work with a person, not against them, in order to achieve their objectives. On several occasions, Josée required hospitalization to manage her bipolar symptoms, and it took repeated attempts to get her admitted. It seems to depend on the day, the doctor, and who knows what other factors.

Why does someone need to be actively suicidal or self-harming before anyone listens? Are hospital staff aware of how much courage it takes for someone to come forward and admit that they need help? Moreover, when that person is accompanied by family members who love and care for them and are obviously concerned about them, how can they not be taken seriously? Don't hospital staff know that caring for a family member with a mental illness can wear out even the strongest of caregivers? Do they recognize that, at some point, our need for respite will be as great as the patient's need for treatment?

We once even brought with us a letter from Josée's psychiatrist describing her manic state and need for hospitalization—and it did nothing to expedite the process. I got to thinking that I might have to pull out the big guns and threaten the hospital staff. Thankfully, I never ended up needing to use a threat, but it's a back-pocket option for future reference.

Oh, the joys and struggles. Some days have more of one, some days more of the other. Thankfully, the intensities change. My kids wake up every day and take their morning pills, reminding themselves of the realities of their disorder and what they require to remain stable. I wake up every morning and the pill I have to swallow is that their reality is mine. I have to dig deep and find the power, and peace of mind, to balance the needs of myself and all my family members, continually looking upwards to the Almighty God who gives me strength.

When dealing with the giant of formal systems—and the professionals who monitor them—the hardest answer to accept is "I don't know." As in, I don't know why your child has this diagnosis, or what may have provoked this episode, or why the meds aren't working. And the hardest prescription to fill is time—time to assess, time to treat, and time to heal.

However, once these words permeate, once the need to know everything is sacrificed, there is peace.

Healing

The cooing of a morning dove, healing with each coo, what a sound. A simple sound, one that can seep through your heart.

—Josée Leclair

16. DIAGNOSIS, THE NECESSARY EVIL

Melody

SOME PEOPLE FRET ABOUT HAVING A LABEL APPLIED TO THEM. However, sometimes you need a label in order to get the available supports. Diagnoses came early for Josée and Luke, as they struggled through elementary school. Their needs became obvious when they were young, and it was clear to more than just us that something might be up. So when they were little, we arranged to have them both meet with a private psychologist for a psycho-educational assessment that essentially tested for strengths and weaknesses in all spheres of life and learning. Ideally these sorts of tests are completed in Grade Three, and repeated in Grade Nine.

The school board also had in-house psychologists who could provide this same service, though often the wait times were horrendous. Josée's results revealed a language-based learning disability and central auditory processing disorder. Luke's revealed a language-based learning disability in the mild range, affecting his ability to read and write. This disability, combined with ADHD and an intense, sensitive, and easily frustrated temperament, exacerbated the issue. The diagnoses led to in-school supports and accommodations.

They initially each got put on an Individual Education Plan, or IEP, and we later formalized the working document through an Identification, Placement, and Review Committee, or IPRC, which was to be reviewed annually. The benefit, of course, was the assurance that its recommendations would be followed through by teachers and support staff.

Interestingly, both Luke and Josée came to be successful academically, in their own ways. Josée, through her love of reading, eventually came to write, and that is now her greatest strength. Luke used technology to enable him to put his thoughts to paper, and he excelled in technological programs, such as the machine shop, and learned to design and build things.

Through our experiences, we have learned that not only can a diagnosis help aid the process of receiving financial support and other services, it can also equip kids with the proper tools and technology to overcome their disabilities.

Once Upon the Unexpected

Do you see what I see? I see a world that
questions if light is even visible. What is the
dissolving point of darkness? Find the twinkles
they say. Fan away the lies. In every truth there
is a flower. When in the midst of it all. I guess
you might as well look for the door in the moon.
Sadness, it is the beginning of wisdom.

—Josée Leclair

17. SERGE'S THERAPEUTIC EMAIL UPDATES

Melody

THROUGHOUT LUKE'S CRISIS, SERGE KEPT OUR FRIENDS AND FAMILY abreast of our situation and reported Luke's progress. It proved to be an effective way of keeping people informed and up to date, and it helped us to gain prayer support and encouragement. Writing the updates also gave Serge the opportunity to reflect, process, and heal from all that was happening.

From· Serge
Sent· Wednesday, February 8, 2017 5·56 PM
Subject· Luke

Dear friends,
I'm writing you this letter as I wait for the transfer vehicle to take Luke to CAIP (Children and Adolescent Inpatient Program) at Grand River in Kitchener. He is in a state of psychosis. Please pray.
Serge and Melody

From· Serge
Sent· Wednesday, February 8, 2017 8·58 PM
Subject· Re· Luke

Thanks for the prayers, everyone. Melody and I just got back from CAIP. When we left, the nurse was trying to get a hold of the on-call psychiatrist to prescribe something to knock him out. We suspect he has not had a solid sleep since Saturday night. He continues to be in varying stages of psychosis and is definitely in a state of mania.

He's in great hands over there. The nurses are great and will give him the attention he needs. At this end, we are keeping a pretty level head. It's a little easier when you understand the system and all the terms. We have a meeting with the social worker tomorrow at 1·00 and should get a better idea of what kind of treatment he will get.

Again, thanks for the prayers and we will keep you posted as things progress.
Serge and Melody

From· Serge
Sent· Thursday, February 9, 2017 4·12 PM
Subject· Re· Luke

Hi everyone,
Just a quick update. Luke is still not great. He did get some sleep but is still very anxious with racing thoughts when he is awake. Our meeting was really more just to gather information… we probably won't know much until Monday. Right now, as hard as this is as parents, the best thing to do is to leave him alone so that he gets the littlest amount of stimulation as possible… us visiting is just making it worse but it is so counterintuitive.

So again, thanks for the prayers and if you don't hear from me in the next couple days it's because not much has changed and I don't really know what to report. Just be comforted in knowing that he's in the best place he can be right now and I'm sure it will all work itself out soon.

Thanks again, everyone!
Serge and Melody

From· Serge
Sent· Wednesday, February 14, 2017 2·32 PM
Subject· Re· Luke

Hello everyone,
I'm happy to report that Luke is not out of the woods, but
he at least knows what direction is out. There are still a lot
of trees, lakes, and mountains, but he's a good camper so
I'm confident he will find his way out.

It was a very hard weekend as we really didn't see any
significant progress until today. Right now, they are still
working on getting him caught up on his sleep and giving
him as little stimuli as possible.

We had a team meeting this morning with all involved in his care. The psychiatrist is confirming that this
is bipolar and now is working on figuring out how this is
going to play out as it will be concurrent with ADHD. He
is nowhere near discharge. They need to get him back to
baseline and also work out the best medication formula.
They are also very aware of Josée's condition and realize
reintegration may be especially hard. With that said, a
long-term three-month facility in London may also be
part of the formula. There they would give him coping
skills on how to live with this disorder.

At this end we are pretty fragile. Melody has taken
a two-week leave from work and my work has been very
understanding by reducing my workload and being very
accommodating with allowing me to take time off to visit
him and meet with doctors. The girls are doing okay. We
just met with the VP at GCVI and he assured us that he
and his team will do everything in their power to make
sure Josée has a successful semester. We are also keeping a

close eye on Karina, but honestly she is enjoying the quiet house. They both have a meeting with the hospital social worker tomorrow so that they can check in and let them know how the hospital can support them as well.

We thank all of you for your continued prayers, phone calls, and visits. The love feels awesome!
Serge and Melody

From· Serge
Sent· Wednesday, February 18, 2017 6·21 PM
Subject· Re· Luke

Hey everyone,
I've added a few more people on this list. Feel free to read the trail. It's easier this way than writing the same thing ten different times.

Luke appears to have made it over a big mountain today; yesterday we met with the psychiatrist, as he felt the drug he was on was not working. We agreed, as yesterday's visit did not go very well. So last night they tried something different and he was much better today. His emotions are very distorted, but at least for the first time in ten days he's starting to think a little clearer.

Attached you will see a couple pictures of his therapy wall. He wanted everyone to know that he is getting better, and if you zoom in you will see that one of the frogs is named Luke and is leaping from "unhealthy" (it is written very faintly under the frog in yellow) to a bright red "healthy."

He misses everyone very much and enjoys reading all the letters he's received when he's feeling sad. So, keep them coming. If you like, feel free to respond to this message with a note for him and I will print it and bring it to him.

Thanks again, everyone, for your thoughts and prayers. They are working!
Serge and Melody

From· Serge
Sent· February 23, 2017 9·45 PM
Subject· Re· Luke

Good evening, Luke followers,
Sorry, I realize it's been a little while since my last update. I was travelling this week so it was a little hectic.

Well, here we are on day fifteen. Melody and I just got back from a visit with Luke. He is slowly coming back into his own. He's back to his charming little self. The nurses love him and enjoy his ease of getting along with everyone. He loves all the rules. I know this sounds weird, but for those of you who know Luke well you will agree that he has always loved rules.

He finally got to visit with his sisters on family day. It was great to have my whole family together on family day. We kept it low-key; Luke was having fun entertaining the girls. They actually missed each other. He was also pretty witty. At one point he was explaining to the girls how bored he was one morning. He had woken up early and couldn't get out until 10·30, so he played tic-tac-toe with himself. Melody proceeded to ask him, "How does that work?" His answer was, "Well, you win an awful lot!"

They continue to monitor him and slightly adjust his meds to find the right combination. They have also formally referred him to the Parkwood Institute in London—we should find out next week if he gets accepted and if they have room. He has started some workbook modules on his disorder and is also getting some group and individual therapy.

At this end we are continuing to try to take it one day at a time and not get too far ahead of ourselves. Melody was actually able to join me for a night while I was at a conference; it was nice, as it felt like a little escape. The girls are also being supported by the hospital with weekly counselling sessions.

We have another team meeting with his circle of care on Monday. We will discuss his therapeutic goals and how the next few days will look like until we find out about Parkwood.

Thanks again for your continue support, thoughts, and prayers!
Serge and Melody

From· Serge
Sent· Wednesday, March 12, 2017 10·12 PM
Subject· Re· Luke

Hey Luke's fan club,

You will notice that you have now all been placed in bcc. This list is getting pretty long, and I was afraid the privacy police might come after me. Also, some of you have asked permission to forward this email chain on. The answer is yes, absolutely. The more people hear about Luke's story the quicker we will win the STIGMA battle.

It will be two weeks tomorrow that Luke is at Parkwood Institute in London, and let me tell you the honeymoon is definitely over. The first few days were good. We talked to him every day and he was in good spirits. Last weekend, he was granted some passes where he was able to go back to Ronald McDonald House with us. He was granted four hours the Friday evening but only lasted two. He lasted three on Saturday and five on Sunday. He has become very anxious and scared of everything. An increased anxiety is a normal symptom, and so is irritability, so we we're not too concerned, but it was very exhausting to be with him. However, we managed to have Melody's parents and her brother's family over on Sunday and he was still able to be the funny cousin in front of the younger ones.

Last week seemed to go okay. He was still very anxious and wasn't sleeping too well, but the nurse's reports didn't seem too concerning. One of his teachers from Guelph visited him on Tuesday and his youth pastor on Thursday; he was pretty pleased and impressed that they would come all this way just to visit him! However, things changed this past Friday when we went for our weekly meeting with the social worker. As of Thursday, Luke had been placed on constant observation (CO). This means there is always a nurse or worker observing him 24/7. Luke's anxiety and irritability had become debilitating, but when the constant observation started it seemed like having a presence there to help regulation everything calmed down. This constant observation was to remain through the weekend, which meant we would only be able to visit him in the ward. This was very disappointing to us, as we were hoping to be able to take him back with us for a few passes like the previous weekend. We made the best of it and visited him twice a day. He could only really last two hours at a time before he got pretty tired. We did have a pretty good visit this afternoon when both sets of grandparents and sisters were there. He was busy touring everybody around and showing all the drawings and different therapy techniques he was learning. Surprisingly he continues to be in good spirits. He maintains a sense of humour about it and looks forward to getting all this sorted out.

Right now, my parents and Josée have taken our place at McDonald House; they will visit him tomorrow evening and Melody will go back midweek. Let me tell you, we are so grateful for the McDonald House. They are a true living example of grace. The staff members know you by name and are compassionate and really make you feel at home. Feel free to have a look for yourself on this virtual tour· http·//www.rmhc-swo.ca/staying-with-us/ ronald-mcdonald-house-london/tour

Melody continues to be off work; in fact, she will be receiving EI sick benefits to extend her time as needed. We are grateful to be able to access supports that we never knew existed for such a time as this. Your continued thoughts and prayers are much appreciated.
Serge

From· Serge
Sent· Wednesday, April 2nd, 2017 8·42 PM
Subject· Re· Luke

Hello everyone,
I realize it's been a few weeks since I gave you an update. As you can imagine, things continue to be very busy for

us. Well, I'm happy to announce that Luke has improved significantly in the past few weeks. He was taken off constant observation after showing signs of mood regulation. He has been coming home weekends and is now able to focus during the school time at the hospital, and he continues to keep a good attitude. As he told me once on one of the drives, "Dad, I really need to take in all of this therapy while in hospital, so I can come back much better." We seem to have found a good med combo that is helping keep his moods regulated. There are still some physical side effects, but the psychiatrist will try an antidote drug to fight some of those this week.

We are also happy to announce that Luke has been given a discharge date of April 12, so if all goes well he will be home for Easter. Our prayer now is that the transition home will be a good one and that school somehow will not be too affected and that they will accommodate for him to get at least a couple credits.

Thanks for your continued love and prayers, and maybe the next and final update will come from Luke himself when he is back home for good!

Many thanks again,
Serge and Melody

From· Serge
Sent· Wednesday, April 30, 2017 6·42 PM
Subject· Re· Luke

A final hello to Luke's prayer warriors!

Well, it's been two and half weeks now since Luke has been home and things are going pretty good. The new normal is settling in just fine. He came home as planned on the 12th, just before Easter. My brother and his family came to visit on Good Friday and he had enough stamina to visit the entire day.

We had a reintroduction meeting with the school VP and social worker where we established a safety plan for Luke in case he was to have a relapse. We also rebuilt his schedule, and surprisingly enough he will likely still manage to get three credits from this semester! We were all quite pleased with that. So far he has attended every day without a hitch. He starts off with a resource class where he is working on the in-class portion of a gym course, followed by actual gym, then drama, and ending with his favourite· machine tech.

The home life is also going pretty well. I would say he and Josée have found a happy medium of tolerance for each other. We also find that his constant chatter has diminished; I guess he learnt in his therapy that it was probably a form of insecurity. So, I would say our new normal feels almost better than it was. Knowing our struggles is half of the problem solved.

So aside from the current weekly psychiatrist appointments, blood work, and us regularly checking in with him to make sure he had a good sleep or that his moods are regular, I would say this has made Luke and our family stronger. A few days ago, Karina even said that what we are going through with Luke and Josée in a way has brought us closer together as a family and community. As we read in Proverbs 3·5–6· "Trust in the LORD with all your heart and lean not on your own understanding; in all your ways submit to him, and he will make your paths straight" (NIV). Although the path still seems crooked, it sure is straighter then it has been in a long time.

So this is a formal farewell in this email chain, but stay tuned as Melody has started writing a book! We also continue to regularly visit with all of you one on one and appreciate the support very much.

Blessings to all,

Serge and Melody

A Secret-Keeper

A fabrication, a secret you may ask—ask away
as I have none, an escaped giggle, a guided move
I intended it this way, it stood motionless, an
unapologetic let out, how worth it was it really,
bringing back the simplicity, a pure voice of
wandering thought, a still candid snapshot, a
slow hit and then all at once, please don't leave
me—a back pocket thought.

—Josée Leclair

18. HIDDEN GEMS

Melody

HIDDEN GEMS ARE OFTEN EMBEDDED IN THE HEART OF TRIALS AND tribulations. There may be no good enough reason to justify one's suffering, but many results come from it. To find the hidden gems, it is essential to lean in, listen to one's pain, and in time discover the beauty that can be made when a person is under fire. These hidden gems lurk beneath the surface, like missed cues that will reveal themselves in the future. It is possible to notice and appreciate them as they happen, but more often than not they are only discovered post-crisis.

One such hidden gem for us has been the healing power of speaking engagements. In the fall of 2014, a friend of the family asked about my willingness to speak about mental health at a church event. Since she was acquainted with our experiences, she boldly asked if I could share from both professional and personal perspectives. I felt compelled to be courageously vulnerable and speak to the realities and complexity of mental health, for my sake and others'.

I didn't have to give it a second thought—except to ask Josée's permission, of course.

"Absolutely," Josée's replied. "But only if I can tell my story myself."

Unbeknownst to me, Josée had already written down her whole experience. It turns out there is a writer in both of us. She told me that she'd done it to help herself put things in perspective and make sense of it. Wow. What a child of God we were blessed with!

This began a series of talks that now include my husband and middle daughter, who share from their perspectives as well. As for Luke, just prior to his episode, and even in the middle of it, he had been thinking of what he would like to contribute based on his experiences.

We have presented at small churches, medium-sized fundraisers, and most recently back-to-back high school assembles where we addressed our largest audience ever of 1,400 staff and students. When asked what we like about this, we tell people that it's not about us sharing our stories as much as it is hearing the stories people share with us, stories of personal experience, trials, and triumph. Untold stories are also communicated through tear-filled eyes, warm embraces, and yes, even standing ovations. These responses speak volumes. They tell me that people are hungry for personal experiences—for people to be real, to put voice to their pain, to relate, and to educate folks in order to help reduce stigma.

I understand that not everyone is wired to do this, but I encourage people to take more risks and share their stories with someone, anyone, so that nobody has to stand alone.

Melody's Professional Talk

Ever wondered what all the buzz is about mental illness? Are you confused about what it is and sceptical about its prevalence in society and how it impacts us and our youth? Perhaps you've even gone so far as to question whether mental illness is real or just in people's heads.

If so, you are not alone. These questions are the beginning of discovery.

My hope for us this morning is that we come with an attitude of curiosity and an open mind to learn more. We'd like to raise awareness today about what mental illness is, who it impacts, and how to support someone who lives with mental illness. Through my family's sharing, we hope at the very least to answer some of your questions, raise new ones, and inspire further conversations that will lead to practical applications.

Let's shed some light on the situation. According to statistics, one in five people will have a mental illness in their lifetime. This means you, or someone you know, has been or will be diagnosed with a mental illness at some point.

According to authors Julia Nunes and Scott Simmie, "There are really only eight kinds of people affected by mental disorders. It's a very small list, so listen closely, we all know someone on it: someone's mother, daughter, sister or wife; someone's father, brother, husband or son."[9]

So why is it that we rush in to support an individual with a broken leg, but shy away from people who have a mental illness? You go for an x-ray and it's black and white. You know how to treat the broken bone, and you know that it will heal. Mental illness is different. It's not a weakness. It's an issue, not an identity.

Recovery is possible. Mental illness isn't always curable, but it is treatable. We need to accept that recovery is a process and that ambiguity is part of the journey. For example, a person with depression may not always look sad, just as a person with bipolar disorder won't always be manic. Symptoms of the same diagnosis may present differently from person to person.

What we need to do is dispel the myths of mental illness and get the facts. In order to accomplish this, we have to talk about it.

It's also important to define what mental health is. According to the World Health Organization, mental health can be described as a state of wellbeing in which a person realizes his or her own abilities, can cope with the normal stresses of life, work productively and fruitfully, and be able to make a contribution to his or her family.

At its heart, mental health is about our ability to respond to challenges. It's also important to recognize that a person's mental health changes over time; today you may feel healthy, but tomorrow you may not.

So what shapes mental health? Research suggests that there are risk factors and protective factors. Some risk factors that negatively impact mental health are poverty, traumatic life experiences, and chronic illness. Protective factors can offset these risk factors and include your ability to complete tasks and reach goals, a supportive family, and strong friends who cushion and support you.

---

9   Julia Nunes and Scott Simmie, *The Last Taboo: A Survival Guide to Mental Health Care in Canada* (Toronto, CA: McClelland & Stewart, 2001), 82.

In essence, mental health is about your ability to cope with stress in healthy ways—and it applies to each one of us. Fostering good mental health means finding balance in all areas of your life: socially, emotionally, physically, spiritually, and mentally.

Mental illnesses, on the other hand, are chronic disruptions in the neural circuits of the brain. The brain is like a huge water system for a thriving metropolis, with millions of pipes that split, weave, and interconnect. In this metaphor, the pipes represent electric chemical signals that pass though the neurons. Having a mental illness would be like if some of the pipes were leaking or clogged so that the water took longer to reach its destination. But through practice you can channel more water through certain pipes and less through others, somewhat overcoming those obstacles. The disrupted neural circuits affect the way the brain functions—how a person thinks, feels, and acts—and can dramatically affect a person's moods and interpretations of life events. The causes of disrupted neural circuits come in many forms: biological factors, environmental factors, or a combination of the two, including genetics, traumatic events, stress, drugs and alcohol, or lack of sleep.

The term "mental illness" refers to a range of concerns. Six of the most common types of mental illness include eating disorders, personality disorders, anxiety and depression, addiction, and psychotic disorders. *The Diagnostic and Statistical Manual of Mental Disorders* contains the complete list of diagnoses that are considered mental illnesses. The authors of this manual note that the psychiatrists, doctors, and therapists who have defined the categories for mental illness struggle with "the term mental disorder [because it] unfortunately implies a distinction between 'mental' disorders and 'physical' disorders."[10] They add that there is much "physical" in mental disorders and much "mental" in physical disorders.

Think about it. Perhaps you've had the misfortune of sustaining a physical injury that kept you from working for a period of time. Sure, you might enjoy the first few days off, but it doesn't take long before you battle to keep your thoughts positive.

---

10 *The Diagnostic and Statistical Manual of Mental Disorders, Fourth Edition* (Washington, DC: American Psychiatric Association, 1994), xii.

On the flipside, have you ever considered the impact of mental stress on your physical body? As humans, we tend to wear our stress. For some people, this results in migraines, a tense neck and shoulders, back pain, etc., and we go to great lengths to treat these symptoms via massage and chiropractic, among other treatments.

The specialists who contributed to *The Diagnostic and Statistical Manual of Mental Disorders* further state, "There is no definition that adequately specifies precise boundaries for the concept of a mental disorder. The concept of a mental disorder, like many other concepts in medicine and science, lacks a consistent operational definition that covers all situations."[11] In other words, while there are diagnoses that best fit what a person is experiencing, this is not a precise science. They conclude that mental illness needs to be considered from behavioural, psychological, and biological perspectives. Psychiatric treatment, effective therapy, peer support, and family support—not to mention the basics, such as sleep, diet, and exercise—are important components in the recovery process.

So why don't we talk about mental health and mental illness? There may be many reasons, but in my opinion the primary one is stigma—a cultural bias that creates a vicious cycle. People seclude themselves and hide in shame because of the unknown thing they are struggling with. It has been said that people coping with mental illness have a lot more to deal with than the disorder itself. Many people report that the stigma of mental illness, and the prejudices they encounter because of it, is nearly as bad as their disorder's actual symptoms.

Thankfully, the tides are changing. We are fortunate to live in a day and age where society acknowledges that mental illness exists. More importantly, society is working towards inclusion rather than segregation.

My hope in coming here today is to confront stigma and help reduce it by talking about it and creating more safe spaces for people. In doing so, we will experience healing, and this is why we have chosen to share our story with you.

---

11 Ibid.

Josée's Talk

My name is Josée. I'm a student, a friend, a sister, a daughter, a writer, a figure skater, a rock climber, and I have bipolar disorder. I'm here to share my experience with mental illness and where I am today in my journey. I grew up in a Christian home, going to church every Sunday and always believing there was a God. I have a great family with a younger brother and sister and two awesome and loving parents.

As I grew older, my world was shaken. In Grades Four and Five, I experienced lots of on and off worry and tears, sometimes without a real reason. When kept inside, these intense feelings turned into physical symptoms resulting in stomach-aches, hot flashes, and poor sleeping habits.

Over time, the symptoms got worse and a battery of physical tests by my doctor revealed the culprit: anxiety. At that point, I started counselling to help me cope.

During the summer of Grade Six, the anxiety really hit me. My parents had planned for me to go away for a month. I was to spend time at camp and visit my aunt and uncle to help them with their kids. That month didn't go as well as we wanted it to. I ended up feeling anxious the whole time, and even depressed.

My feelings of anxiety and depression continued into Grades Seven and Eight. I struggled with either feeling too much or nothing at all. Then, in the spring of Grade Eight, I started to experience highs and lows. During the highs, I was full of energy, talking a mile a minute, overly happy all of the time. I said things that didn't make sense and that were very unlike me. I was impulsive and didn't sleep for weeks but still had tons of energy. It was almost like a living dream, and I didn't know what was real.

I would then sink into lows during which I'd feel very depressed. I wouldn't feel like doing anything. I felt like I was carrying weights, not necessarily knowing why, and in these times I even had suicidal thoughts. This was a cry for help, as I knew no other way to express myself and my confusion.

But then I would bounce back into a high. The cycle continued through the spring right through to July. My life got a little wild, and my parents became concerned, along with friends, neighbours, and teachers.

One day, during one of my high periods, everything changed. My friend went to a baseball game, and for some reason I had the sudden urge to tell him something right away. I wasn't thinking clearly, so I hopped on my bike and decided to find out where the game was. I rode with incredible speed. At one point, I stopped, looked around, and realized that I was in front of a good friend's house—a completely different friend than the person I had been going to see.

Suddenly, I knew something was wrong. I walked up and knocked on the door while crying uncontrollably. When her mom saw me, she right away pulled me into a hug, then sat me down with her husband and daughter as she called my parents. It helped that my friend's mom was also my teacher from school.

My friend's parents suggested that I go to the hospital because something was going on mentally. My mom came and took me to the hospital. I thank my friend's parents greatly, as everything would have played out differently if they hadn't been home. In fact, I'd almost missed them at the time since they had just been about to leave for the grocery store. I am very grateful they were there for me.

I ended up spending the night at the hospital. Throughout the night, I was incoherent. I also thought that I was seeing and hearing things. My parents stayed with me the whole time.

It was decided that night that in the morning I would go to the Child and Adolescent Inpatient Psychiatry Program at Grand River General Hospital in Kitchener. While there, I went from experiencing highs to being super angry, crying, and swearing. After being there for eight days, I was diagnosed with bipolar disorder.

My parents decided it would be for the best if they took me someplace where I felt comfortable, so we went camping. But it went a bit differently than our usual camping trips, which was to be expected. I ended up sleeping a ton and crying a lot. I would sleep all night, wake up, have breakfast, then go back to sleep, wake up, have lunch, and go back to sleep. I cried whenever I was awake, realizing all the ridiculous things I had done and said and trying to figure out what was going to happen next and what people would think of me. I questioned God about why I was like this and how this could be part of his plan. My faith wavered a lot. I had to keep reminding myself to have hope—hope that I would come out of this, hope that there was a reason and purpose, and hope that he was taking care of me.

In Grade Nine, I had three hypomanic episodes, which are a tame version of mania. This led to more questioning. My psychiatrist explained that some people with bipolar disorder can go decades without experiencing a blip. That's what I wanted for my life.

One day I came across a poem that I felt related to my own feelings: "Footprints in the Sand" by Mary Stevenson. The poem talked about walking along the sand with God, looking back, and sometimes only seeing one set of footprints. When she questioned God about this, he told her that he hadn't left her in those times; rather, he had been carrying her.

The poem made me realize that God really was taking care of me, and caring for me. He had put supportive and understanding people in my life. I realized that no one ever bothered me about the things that had happened. God was making me stronger and helping me to gain from my experiences.

I pondered these thoughts for a while and out popped a poem that I called "Pain, Loss, Regret." It goes like this:

Pain, loss, regret what do these three powerful words mean?
Why do we feel these three common words?
"Pain" pain from past, pain from loss, pain from burdens, pain.
"Loss" loss of yourself, loss of who you were, loss of someone, loss.
"Regret" regret of situations, regret of actions, regret of words, regret.

What do these words mean to you? For me, they mean hope—the hope to replace these words with another one: gain. I want to gain from the things I've learned in the past, from the losses I've had, from the burden I once held. I want to gain from the loss of myself, from the person I once was, from losing someone who was close to me. I want to gain from regret, the regret of situations, regret of actions, and regret of words. The question is not what you've lost, but what you've gained from it. It's about the person you've become. There is hope.

"Footprints in the Sand" helped me to let go and believe that there was more. Sometimes when you're in the middle of a struggle, it's hard to gain perspective about what's going on. This is why my family and I have needed the help of others to step back and get a clear perspective.

Know that there is a bigger picture and that there is hope. Don't stop believing.

Melody's Personal Talk

Josée is a fun-loving person who is always up for a good adventure. She loves nature and could climb from the time she could walk. I have vivid memories of her on tabletops, rooftops, and treetops. This no doubt contributed to her nick name: Monkey. To this day, it's not uncommon to find Josée nestled up in a tree reading a book. She loves to camp, rock-climb, and travel near and far. Her beautiful smile lights up a room, and in spite of her challenges she embodies a quiet confidence in faith and life that inspires others.

So you can well imagine the shock we felt as parents facing our baby girl's diagnosis. No amount of psychology training, work experience, or parenting could have ever prepared us for the trauma of witnessing our child not being herself. Josée is the eldest child of three, and up until the time of her crisis it was difficult to judge what was normal and what wasn't. Mood swings, lethargy, and spurts of energy seem to go with the territory of being a teenager. What we have come to understand is that the presence of these symptoms does not lead to a diagnosis; the frequency, intensity, and duration of the symptoms do.

They say that hindsight is twenty-twenty. Looking back, we can honestly say that we saw the signs. We witnessed periods of ups and downs, and soon it became obvious even to those outside the family. It takes a community to raise a child, and our experience demonstrates this. Concerned teachers, parents, youth pastors, and neighbours began to dialogue with us about Josée's changes, voicing genuine concern. We are so very grateful to be surrounded by such a caring community that wasn't afraid to speak into our lives without casting judgment on Josée or ourselves.

What may not have been obvious in Josée's account is the role suicidal thoughts played in getting her help. She first posted her thoughts of suicide on a group chat of which her youth pastor was a part; he quickly assessed whether she was at risk of imminent harm and then immediately got a hold of us. In the meantime, that day she knocked on her teacher's door was her moment of desperation. She rang the doorbell, opened the door, announced that she wanted to die, and collapsed from exhaustion.

Up until then, Josée couldn't articulate the confusion that had been playing out in her head, and the only way to stop the pain, in her mind, was to die. Simultaneously, a concerned neighbour showed up on my doorstep to ask about Josée's unusual behaviour. It was at this point that help was imminent. I was advised to take her to the ER, where a lengthy process began of evaluating her and then admitting her to CAIP.

These were dark and difficult days for our family, for what happened to Josée happened to all of us. There was an emotional toll to pay. To make sense of our experiences, we opened ourselves to individual and family counselling. As badly as I wished Josée would have come to me, I understand why she didn't. It would have been all too real for both of us. My "mother's guilt" may have overtaken my ability to respond in the way I would have wanted, the way I had been trained to respond. There's a reason therapists don't counsel friends and family. The closer the family member, the less objective one can be.

In my experience of counselling, it's common for people who have depression to experience thoughts of suicide. A person's pain limits their vision. If they can't talk about it, they will act on it. I've never heard of anyone talking themselves to death. When people come into my office and speak about their thoughts of suicide, I am grateful. Why? Because as long as they're talking, there is hope.

Months after the initial shock of our daughter's crisis, diagnosis, and hospitalization, I became overwhelmed with emotions: sadness, denial, and fear. I felt as though I was experiencing depression myself. In time, I came to understand this as an experience of grief. I had much to grieve. Everything had changed, for better or worse. Although I hadn't lost a child to death, I had lost a child to the life I had envisioned. I came to see the futility of magical thinking, the idea that as parents we can keep our children from all harm, and I confronted my sense of helplessness and perceived loss of control. I grieved the person my daughter had been, and the mother I used to be.

Accepting Josée's diagnosis meant confronting my own biases, beliefs, and assumptions about mental health. You may not know you have these sorts of biases until you're affected by mental illness. For me, this included the cultural stigma of silence and shame, and disbelief that this could be happening to her, to me, to us.

I also had to contend with the myth that faith grants us immunity from pain. Where was God in the midst of all this? Carrying us through. In people, in spirit, in word, and in deed.

As we shared our pain, people shouldered our burdens. Meals, prayers, cards, and visits sustained us during the uncertainty of crisis, and in time this helped bring us to a place of hope.

Know that there is life after diagnosis. Understanding the problem is half the solution. Things can change and get better. We can adapt and do things differently. New dreams are possible.

Developing a circle of care is the byproduct of investing in relationships—sometimes it benefits others, and other times it benefits you. The caring community around us meant early detection and diagnosis, leading to good inpatient treatment and outpatient care.

Our family has been amazed by the availability of mental health supports such as Trellis's mobile health unit (available through CMHA and Here 24/7), crisis workers, counsellors, psychiatrists, mental health nurses, and in-school social workers.

With our willingness to trust the process and allow professional involvement, the quality of Josée's life and ours has significantly improved. Experiencing a crisis drives one to consider what is most important, and surrender quickly follows. Before long, with supports in place, everything in our lives resumed, although we had to get used to the new normal.

Today, apart from ongoing psychiatric care, medication, and regular blood work, Josée is living life to the fullest. She enjoys figure skating, rock-climbing, photography, writing, and being in nature. She hopes to make writing her career.

As parents, we are learning that mental illness doesn't need to have the last say. As we accept the reality of our situation, so too can we empower ourselves and others to find the courage to fight through and talk about what is going on so that nobody has to stand alone.

Luke's Talk

When I was twelve years old, I remember coming home from a sleepover and Josée was playing outside. I went to go give her a hug, and her first words were, "Why did you come back?" My heart sank. I was in complete shock and started to cry.

That night, we had a family meeting without Josée where my mom and dad explained that she was unwell, and they would be taking her to the hospital. Up until that point, we had all been experiencing a side of Josée we had never seen. At least I felt assured that I wasn't the only one who felt this way. I remember wondering if my sister would ever be the same again. This made me feel lost.

As the days, weeks, months, and now years have gone by, it's exhausting to keep seeing her when she is sick, because every time we think we have picked up coping tools, the face of bipolar disorder keeps changing. However, there are things that work, like having family conversations during or after episodes, limiting sibling interactions, and trying not to be reactive to her. When these things fail, I hit the eject button—and go to my grandparents.

My grandma and grandpa's house is a place I consider my second home. My Grandma Martin always makes my favourite meals and we bake and quilt together. Grandpa and I go to McDonald's for breakfast and we hang out with his coffee club, which I am a part of.

And on the other side there is my Grandmama Madeleine, with whom I like to sit on the porch and banter about random things just because we both like to debate. Of course, everything is said and done in the name of fun. She spoils me rotten with junk food, ice cream, and black liquorice. Popsi and I like to be active by going fishing, doing gardening, and talking politics. My visits always prove to be a good distraction from everything happening on the home front.

But all good things must come to an end, and I eventually I'd have to go back home.

Josée always apologizes for the things she has said and done, which doesn't soften the initial blow. Although things have gotten better between Josée and me, there is still lots of room for improvement. We don't always see eye to eye, and at the time I certainly did not understand her disorder. For that reason, my mom set up an appointment for me to see Josée's psychiatrist, Dr. Edwards, for the sole purpose of her explaining the disorder to me.

When I went into this meeting, I noticed that her office had a room full of fidget toys and really cool chairs. She explained bipolar disorder to me and allowed me to ask questions. Little had I known that this information would prove to be very relevant to my own life.

As the meeting went on, she showed me a diagram which demonstrated the way in which Josée's emotions were like a rollercoaster, with big ups and downs. It satisfied my curiosity and explained that Josée wasn't always in control of everything she said and did. It was kind of like trying to control a monster that temporarily would take over her body and mind.

I could relate to this imagery in some ways, since I had been diagnosed with ADHD when I was eight years old. Throughout the years, I'd learned a lot about what makes me unique and gained helpful coping skills.

A doctor once explained my brain chemistry to me. The way I understand it, one side of the brain is high energy and the other side of the brain is low energy. The one side of the brain is trying to wake up the other side of the brain, which produces excess energy. Then, when the two lobes try to communicate, they butt heads, so to speak. This causes me to get distracted. My medication is a stimulant that helps balance out my energy levels.

However, I began struggling with my mental health in a new way during Grade Eight, and I eventually started to see Josée's psychiatrist regularly. She did an assessment and suspected that bipolar disorder may also be the culprit for me. I remember feeling confused and thinking that I wasn't at all like Josée. After all, my symptoms were different.

But this past winter, I underwent a manic episode which confirmed my diagnosis. I was in the hospital for a total of sixty-three days in total, from the beginning of my ER stay all the way to the end of my long-term care.

I wish I had more time to tell you about the wonderful nurses and staff who looked after me, like Matt and Kiel, who saw through my disorder and provided me comfort. Or I could tell you about the mind games the disorder played on me, leading me to believe that the nurses were cutting holes in my socks. Or I could speak of the boredom that drove me to play tic-tac-toe against myself.

In any event, my dad knew I was getting better when my wit and charm started coming back—and life has since returned to a new normal. I have lots of support and am future-oriented. I like to concentrate on my abilities and my future rather than dwell on how my life will never be the same again.

I am forever grateful to have been born into an understanding family. Without their support, I would not be where I am today.

Know that you are not alone. Your experiences will be unique to you. Episodes don't last forever. Time passes, and things change and get better. Hold strong.

Serge's Talk

I will always remember one particular evening in 2013. It was the end of July and I was having dinner with a friend in Toronto when Justin, our kids' youth pastor, texted me to tell me that Josée needed attention immediately, that she was having suicidal thoughts. You may think it was impersonal of him to text me about such a crisis! Well, that was because he was having multiple text conversations; he was staying in touch with Josée, and also trying to text Melody.

By this time, Josée had made it to the house of a friend, who happened to be the daughter of her teacher. They looked after Josée and tried to calm her down while connecting with Melody as well. I managed to get a hold of Melody and found out that Josée was now in the car with her. I was to meet them at the hospital.

Melody had also made arrangements for a family friend, Amanda, to meet her at the hospital so she would have someone to hold her up until I got there, since I was still over an hour away.

When I got there, Amanda didn't go home; instead she went to our house to be with our other two children! The rest of the evening and night consisted of a series of interviews with various members of the hospital staff. All the while, Josée was continuing to be in what we now know as a state of mania. In the middle of the night, we got word that there was a bed available at the children's psych ward in Kitchener and they would transfer her right away.

The next eight days consisted of a series of appointments with nurses, social workers, and psychiatrists. We had to experiment with different drugs as Josée had calmed down a bit, although she still experienced various degrees of mania. The psych ward felt like a jail; her room was bare so that she wouldn't be able to harm herself, there were monitoring cameras everywhere, and we were only allowed to see her for short periods of time. Although it was very hard, I somewhat understood the reasons for those measures.

Near the final days of her stay, we met with the psychiatrist and he announced that it was very likely that Josée had bipolar disorder. They had finally brought her back down with medication, and the diagnosis would be confirmed if her mania was followed by a deep depression. We had planned a family camping holiday, which the doctor felt would be a good environment for Josée to work through the depression in the comfort of her family, away from friends.

Sure enough, during our holiday came a deep depression.

It was now official: Josée had bipolar disorder. What would this mean for us and our family? What would her everyday life look like? What would her future look like? I worried about her sister Karina, the younger sister who often needed to take the role of the older one. Her brother Luke was confused and didn't know what to say or think.

As time went on, and Josée experienced more highs and lows, I found myself very confused about which parts of Josée's personality were authentically her. I wished she could find a happy medium.

So I started researching and reading everything I could find. I had to become an expert on bipolar disorder, even though I didn't make the salary of a psychiatrist! This helped me understand and empathize a little with what Josée was going through.

I must say, the times of depression are the worst. I was raised by an overly positive mother who always motivated us kids into doing things. Well, there's no use in trying that with someone who is depressed; you'll just be throwing salt on the wound.

One great thing my mom always said was that life is all about balance. That's just it: Josée needed to be a balanced individual like all of us, but she needed a few different tools, like medication, counselling, spirituality, and community. This is now our new normal, a constant flux of trial and error to find that balance. Again, it's not much different from what we all do.

This past February, I was in Montreal on business when I got a call from Melody at 5:30 a.m. that another manic episode was upon us—but this time it concerned our youngest child, Luke, who was fifteen at the time. When it happened to Josée, I had only been an hour away, but this time I was seven hours away. With Josée, my drive home from Toronto had felt like a lifetime, whereas my seven-hour drive this time was less stressful. I was able to stay level-headed while Melody texted me the play-by-play. The terms were familiar to me—triage, form one, psychiatric assessment—making it easier to remain calm.

It reminded me of the experience of our first child being born versus the pregnancies for our subsequent kids. With our first, everything was unknown and felt like an emergency. It seemed like we needed to break speed records to get to the hospital on time. With our second, I clearly remember taking the time to do a Tim Hortons run before going to the hospital, as I knew we had time and we had a long night ahead of us.

Similarly, when I got the news about Luke, I didn't race to get to the hospital. I drove safely and knew just what to do. When this had happened to Josée, I'd been surprised at how amped she was, telling me about her recent conversations with Bethany Hamilton, a motivational speaker and surfer from Hawaii. I remember arguing with Josée that there was no way she could have been talking to her. I know now that it's ineffective and inadvisable to argue with someone in psychosis. So with Luke, I was well prepared to go along with his story. I even came up with questions to validate his experience.

By noon that day, I had arrived at the hospital and been told that Luke had been placed on a form one—an involuntary stay—and accepted to be transferred to CAIP. I told Melody to go home, get some rest, and advise the girls of Luke's status. I would remain with him until we got word that a bed had opened up.

It happened very quickly. By 3:00 p.m., the transfer vehicle had shown up, the attendants had strapped him on the stretcher, and off they'd taken him. Again, I remember having been very distraught when I saw the attendants strap Josée onto the stretcher. This time I knew it was protocol. I even remember warning Luke to be prepared. I made a joke so Luke wouldn't resist it.

I then knew that I had to go home and pack him a bag. I was aware of the hospital rules, that I wouldn't be able to bring anything with draw-strings, technology, or sharp objects of any sort.

So off we went to meet him at CAIP. Walking in, I was very pleased to recognize one of the senior nurses who had been very calming for Josée. We went through the motions, got him admitted, saw him for a few min-utes, then went back home with appointments to return the next day to meet with the social worker and psychiatrist.

When we met the psychiatrist, he had a resident working with him. They expressed frustration over their trouble finding the right medication to bring Luke down from his manic state. He had now been high for over twenty-four hours in the hospital, and who knew how many days leading up to it. The resident psychiatrist also expressed confusion, as Luke kept coming in and out of clarity about what was happening, which was very abnormal. We explained that he had a sister with bipolar disorder and had been exposed to the ups and downs, perhaps informing his clarity and awareness. I asked them if that was usual. Neither had any other experi-ence treating siblings. I remember feeling very anxious. For the first time in this ordeal, I had taken a foot into unfamiliar territory.

After meeting with the social worker, we found out that Luke had tried to have lunch with other patients. Since he wasn't able to be surrounded by people, they decided to put him in isolation. With Josée, we had seen other kids in isolation, but Josée had never required this. All of a sudden this new situation felt very severe. They didn't know what meds to use and had no experience treating siblings with bipolar.

Melody and I went our separate ways that afternoon, but I recall our discussion when we got home. We realized that we would need to take the upper hand with the system and put our emotions aside in order to advocate for our children effectively. We pushed for Luke to be placed in a long-term care facility called Parkwood. Sixty-three days later, Luke was ready to come home. And, knock on wood, he has not relapsed.

Melody and I struggle to understand why this happened to us. Indeed, why does it happen to anyone? We strive to overcome guilt, shame, and stigma by doing what we are doing today. By being open, we hope to raise awareness and educate people about the prevalence of mental illness and the fact that it doesn't discriminate.

Faith has certainly been a resource for us, but it doesn't spare us from pain. But looking at Luke fuels me, reminding me that victory can be achieved. He has been exposed to mental illnesses from such a young age. As we waited in the transfer car, I recall him saying, "Don't worry, Dad. They'll look after me and fix whatever is wrong up there." For him, it was no different than going to get a broken leg fixed up—and why would there be stigma in that?

Lastly, Josée is more than her disorder. She is a wonderful self-advocate who knows what she needs and can articulate it. Our earliest memories are of her demonstrating kindness, friendliness, sweetness, and empathy to a fault. I remember one particular occasion when Josée was four and I told her it was time to leave a park. She said, "We can't, Daddy. I haven't made a friend yet." In my estimation, Josée lives the quote by William Butler Yeats: "There are no strangers here, only friends you haven't met yet."

During manic episodes, her innate kindness comes out in the most beautiful ways. I recall the time when Josée got out of the car and said hello to a teenager on the street. I asked her if she knew that boy and she said no. "He just looked like he needed a hello," she said. Who knew what that boy was going through that day? That's just her empathetic way. The impact she has on people gives me hope and helps explain why she is the way she is. She has always shown determination to do and be her best in all circumstances.

And then there is our little Luke, who can cure anybody with one of his hugs. His loving and sensitive nature is admired by many. He will talk to everyone and anyone without judgment. He loves working in the metal shop and aspires to be a great metal worker one day. This gives me confidence that together we will overcome.

Karina's Talk

As you already know, I am the middle child of the family—between siblings with mental illness. I could be considered a young caregiver, essentially meaning someone who cares for family members and is often forced to grow up early and take on more responsibilities.

As a kid, I idolized my sister. Whatever she did, I did. We were best friends. As I got older, though, I grew into my own person. At times when my older sister really struggled, I tried to take on her role; I would work really hard in school, and in and around the house, and do whatever I could to feel helpful. Through the years, I stopped seeing her as the older sister I once idolized; I lost sight of who she still was.

The summer after my sister's diagnosis, I went to summer camp for a program called Advanced Camper Experience (ACE). It was held for the last year of campers before they went on to be leaders. In this program, we went on a two-day camping trip and made some amazing friends. At the end of the week, one of the leaders shared her life story. She'd had a very similar experience to Josée, struggling with a severe mental disorder. Through her story, I had flashbacks of all that had happened to my sister that past year. After my leader was done talking, I couldn't stop crying.

Later that night, she came to talk to me, and I opened up and shared my story. After that, I had an amazing walk back with my friends with lots of rich conversations about faith and God.

The next morning, I talked to my leader's sister about her experience and how she had dealt with it. She told me that at times it had been really tough, but she felt it was important not to lose sight of God's plan.

After that summer, I really matured in my faith and was able to process all that had happened to my sister.

Soon after, I went on a weeklong trip to Belize with my best friend, and I had the time of my life exploring and having fun adventures! When I got home, though, my sister was in the hospital. I can't say I hadn't expected it—before I left, she had seemed unwell—but it didn't change the disappointment. She was gone for close to a month, in and out of different hospitals. During this time, I wanted to know what she was going through and what she was feeling. I couldn't imagine being where she was, so I was left not knowing how to feel.

Luckily, at the time I was part of an amazing program called CELP, or Community Environmental Leadership Program. I shared what was going on with a few friends and my teacher, and they were able to support me; I have no idea what I would have done without them.

Eventually, I got through it and realized that I will never stop looking up to her. Just because she has experienced great challenges doesn't mean she's a different person. She will always be my beautiful, talented, free-spirited, outgoing, older sister.

On the flip side, my brother's situation is completely different. As my brother got older, we fought more and more often. We were completely different from each other, and I didn't understand why he was so sensitive to little things. Slowly but surely, I learned to give him empathy and not to fight, to swallow my pride and be the bigger person. Along the way I have also reached out to a guidance counsellor at my school who supports me.

As you can see, it doesn't matter whether you talk to a guidance counsellor, a teacher, or a camp counsellor. As long as you feel comfortable with them and they can help, that's what matters.

I think what I've learned through this experience is that there is no simple solution to mental illness. You've just got to get through it as best you can with God's help. Our family's experiences have certainly given me a new perspective on life.

All It Needed

It began with a thought, that's all it took,
Encompassing all, shuffling back and forth
Watching from afar, I tip toe closer
At first glance, it appeared wound up
I unstring it with delight, twirling in glee
To the rhythm as it unravels on the spot, I'm
wind taken
It's fire breathing, I take it for a rooftop dance
Back and forth, relaying a story
Making pictures slip through my mind, I'm
haunted by the thought
It would lay underground where it struggles to
see the light.

—Josée Leclair

19. MORE HIDDEN GEMS

Melody: The Story of Luigi

In the fall of 2016, just months prior to Luke's crisis, he was attending CELP, a school-based program that takes students outside the classroom walls and enables them to earn four credits through experiential learning. The experience includes a canoe trip, preparing and serving weekly community meals, and a module that's completed on a bike.

Luke, being our third child and only boy, often received hand-me-down bikes. He didn't think the one he had would be sufficient for CELP, and since his birthday was coming up he boldly requested a new bike. Serge and I thought this was a reasonable request. Luke ended up with a shiny five-hundred-dollar bike he was very proud of. It was a little pricier than what we had originally intended, but we felt it was well-deserved. Luke spent the summer breaking in the bike in advance of his course.

One day, during CELP's biking module, the students finished their outing and Luke placed his bike securely in the bike racks provided. The class had just reconvened for lunch when Luke saw someone trying to cut his lock and steal the bike. He immediately started yelling and screaming, asserting his rightful possession and waving his fists in the air. Luke's teacher also chimed in, and together they chased the culprit, first by foot, then by car.

Unfortunately, the thief, unfazed by their reaction, simply cut the lock and rode away. Although Luke and his teacher never did catch the thief, they sure gave him a run for his money.

Luke was devastated, although he did his best not to show it to his peers. Perplexed by the situation, he stewed about it for the remainder of the afternoon and conjured up a plan to search the immediate community.

Unbeknownst to us, when class let out he decided to canvas the neighbourhood by going door to door, both to ask if anyone had seen his shiny new red bike—or better yet, the thief who had stolen it—and to warn people to secure their belongings.

On this fateful day, as Luke approached a home, the owner was on his porch. Luke, obviously distraught and determined, asked the elderly gentleman about his bike and the thief. The man's son, Luigi, happened to be visiting from out of town and was within earshot. Luigi approached, introduced himself, and told Luke that the gentleman on the porch was his dad. He also told Luke that his sister lived next door. That must have been enough to convince Luke of Luigi's trustworthiness, because when Luigi compassionately offered to drive Luke around the neighbourhood to search for his bike, Luke agreed.

At the end of their unsuccessful search, Luigi asked Luke how he was going to get home and offered him a ride. Since Luke didn't have his bike, or bus fare, he accepted. Serge and I weren't home when our precious cargo was safely delivered, although we are eternally grateful that he was!

But this isn't where the story ends.

Later in the evening, while Serge and I were still out, Luigi returned to our front doorstep. He and Luke had a short but meaningful exchange, which ended with Luigi offering Luke one hundred dollars to help cover the replacement cost of purchasing a new bike. As this was going on, Luke noted to us later, Luigi's wife remained in the car and watched the connection unfold.

You can well imagine the shock Serge and I felt when we returned from work and Luke recounted the details of the day. Our minds immediately went to all the worst-case scenarios—such mixed emotions, thoughts, and vivid images of what might have happened. We shared our joys and concerns with Luke, and reminded him of all the lessons we had taught him regarding stranger danger. What had he been thinking?

To Luke, the thing that mattered most had been getting his bike back, seemingly at any cost. We were left with a nagging doubt that there may be some ulterior motive by Luigi other than altruism.

Serge and I weren't sure if we should try and get in touch with Luigi. We let it sit for weeks and didn't take any action, but our son would not let us forget. To Luke, his and Luigi's chance encounter had been destined.

Now, let me backtrack. In the conversation Luke and Luigi had on the front porch, Luigi had empathized with Luke over his stolen possession and shared that he, too, had experienced a loss. He told Luke about the death of his son, also named Luke, a few years prior when he had been around our Luke's age. Our son took Luigi's story to heart and even shared it as a prayer request at church.

Weeks later, Serge drove Luke to the house where Luke and Luigi had met to deliver a token of appreciation. Luke entrusted a treasured possession to Luigi's niece, a collectable coin, and requested that she give it to Luigi. At the same time, Luke asked for Luigi's phone number so that we could thank him for the sum of money.

Days later, Luke initiated a phone call while Serge and I remained on standby.

By this time, we felt it necessary to give Luigi the benefit of the doubt and extend an invitation for tea so that we could meet him and his wife and thank them in person. Sure enough, they accepted. I must admit, I was a little nervous and anxious about what to expect. The minute the doorbell rang and I saw Luigi and his wife Shelagh, I felt at ease. You could see love in their eyes.

As we began to unpack all that had happened, we shared genuine honesty of the rarest kind. Luigi said that, upon initially meeting Luke, he had connected to his passion and pursuit to get back what had been lost. Luigi also shared how he had been deeply moved to receive Luke's thank-you coin, since his own son had also owned a collection. Talk about a spiritual connection.

The next hours passed like minutes as we took turns sharing our perspectives on what had happened. Serge and I asked about their son and family and how they were moving through their grief. We laughed, we cried, and there began a kindred friendship.

Since then, Luke and Luigi have met up several times, whether it's for breakfast, a house call, or a chat over the phone. Luigi and Shelagh are now an important part of Luke's life and ours. They have been a support to us throughout Luke's crisis, and they serve as a testament to the fact that strangers are just friends we haven't yet met. Having strangers empathize with our son taught us how to better empathize with others, regardless of their circumstances.

Melody: Work as a Psychotherapist

There is no good time for a crisis, but when I consider how ours played out, I'm awestruck at the timing of it. Back in 2016, I made the decision to fold my private practice, giving up my clientele and contracts as well as letting go of my involvement with bereavement groups—all of which I had enjoyed—in order to accept fulltime employment with a counselling agency.

It was a hard decision, but a good one, as it provided me with regular hours, a salary, and benefits. Little did I know that this is precisely what my family and I would require to stay afloat financially amidst an unexpected crisis. You see, to be eligible for Employment Insurance in Ontario, you must have fifty-two weeks of insurable hours. When Serge and I did the math, my hours served just met that criteria. I had started full-time work on February 1, 2016, and Luke became ill on February 8, 2017, providing me with fifty-three weeks of insurable income.

Unbeknownst to us, my agency provided a sub-plan top-up, bringing my salary close to ninety percent, as opposed to the fifty-five percent that EI provides.

Serge: Mining for Gems

Last Christmas, before leaving for our annual Leclair family cottage trip, I walked up the stairs and noticed that the ceiling had a yellow crack in it. Now, our house is over one hundred years old and there are cracks everywhere, but I know that when there is discolouration around the cracks, you need to worry. I touched the ceiling and it was spongy, indicating that the drywall was wet. Since the bathroom was directly above, I quickly started looking for some kind of pipe leak. Sure enough, I found the smallest leak I had ever seen from one of the faucet pressure pipes.

What was I to do, given that we were scheduled to leave the next morning? I decided to shut the water off and deal with it when we got back. If the water was off, it couldn't get any worse. I just hoped that upon our return the ceiling wouldn't be on the floor.

Thankfully, everything was still intact upon our return home. I don't like doing patch jobs, and the phrase that most often gets my line of credit in trouble is "while I am at it." This was no exception. I never liked the layout of the bathroom anyhow, so I told Melody and the kids to go have their last shower, as I didn't know when they would be able to shower again. A scary proposition.

After they had showered, I ripped the shower down to its studs. I did get the shower functioning again within a week, but it was just a working shower in the corner, with the rest of the bathroom still in shambles. We had to live amidst this renovation chaos in our only full bathroom.

I plugged away—no pun intended—on evening and weekends, and was about halfway through the job when Luke went into crisis.

As a "typical man," when I see a problem, I think I can just fix it—and I always attempt to do so, whether I have the necessary expertise or not. In my kids' cases, although I have acquired quite a bit of knowledge in the mental health field, I have to accept that sometimes I just can't fix it. No one can.

But I kept working away at the bathroom, in order to be able to fix something tangible.

Unfortunately, that type of therapy can get expensive, so another resource for me is Psalm 46:10—"*Be still, and know that I am God*" (NIV). Sometimes you just have let things play out; don't always try to fix it, as hard as that can be sometimes.

In 2013, when Josée was first admitted to the hospital, I was a sales executive for a big company out of Chicago. My superiors were compassionate about my situation, but they didn't give me any more leeway than they had to. I basically took one day off as a personal day. At that time, Melody was able to take a couple months off to help Josée get back on her feet.

The following summer, I had a new manager and we just didn't see eye to eye, so they decided to package me out. At first, I was pretty devastated, but when I picked up Josée from summer camp the next day, high as a kite, I figured out why being packaged out could become a blessing in disguise. Melody's counselling career was just taking off and it was now my turn to look after Josée.

A few months later, I was working again, this time for a much smaller local company, and Josée was doing well.

However, after I'd been with the new company for just eight months, Josée had another episode. I took charge again, as I was on the road and able to flex my schedule. But when Josée attempted suicide and ended up at the hospital on a Friday morning, I had to interrupt a conference call from the office. Everything came to light and I had to let the owners in on what was going on at home. They were very understanding, and I basically worked from home and the hospital until Josée was well again; their compassion was night and day compared to how my other company had handled it.

Fast-forward six months and I was being sought after by another company. When the offer came, it wasn't much more than my current compensation, so I decided to discuss my options with my boss, just to let him in on what was going on. I was glad that he convinced me to stay. One of the things he said was that I needed to keep in mind how the company helped employees when their families fell on rough times. I kind of shrugged that off at the time, as Josée was well and had been for some time. Little did I know that just a few months later I would need help again when Luke fell ill.

The other very cool thing about my work environment is that a majority of my clientele is Dutch, and a lot of Dutch people seem to be Christians. A short time after Luke went into the hospital, I was at a conference and it was obvious to my close clients that I was distraught. I decided to share with them what I was going through, and many of them started praying for me.

One time a client texted me to say that he was thinking about me and wondered how my family was. I placed him on my prayer chain, along with a few other of my clients.

It feels great when your employer realizes that a happy home produces a much more productive worker and gives you the leeway to keep it happy!

Silence

Close your eyes, breathe in, what do you hear?
The wind swaying? The birds singing, the leaves
rolling. Open your eyes. What do you see?
Branches waving to you? The clouds passing
through, the sun piercing through the branches.
What do you feel? The tickling grass? The soft
soil as it trickles through your fingers, or the
rough bark of a tree. The things you can discover
when your senses are alive.

—Josée Leclair

20.
THE
UPS AND DOWNS
OF PARENTING:
WHAT IS NORMAL,
WHAT IS NOT?

Melody

Stats reveal that one in five people will experience mental illness in his or her lifetime, so it shouldn't have come as too much of a surprise to me when this was the experience of not only one of our family members, but two. I do, however, prefer to say that mental health affects five in five. Amongst youth, it's estimated that ten to twenty percent are affected by a mental illness or disorder, and in Canada only one of five children who need mental health services will receive them.

That begs the question: why? Is mental illness more prevalent today? Or has it existed all along but was never recognized—or, more likely, never acknowledged? It is an accepted opinion that many geniuses in history, such as Albert Einstein, Van Gogh, and Shakespeare, struggled with mental illness. In their day, the treatment was to segregate, institutionalize, and use aggressive methods like shock therapy to "snap them out of it."

Today we know that these weren't effective methods.

For hundreds of years, science led us to believe that brains were hardwired. Norman Doidge, M.D, writes in *The Brain That Changes Itself,*

> The common wisdom was that after childhood the brain changed only when it began the long process of decline; that when the brain cells failed to develop properly, or were injured, or died, they could not be replaced. This offered little hope for people who were born with brain or mental limitations. After

years of advances and scientific research we now know otherwise. Neuroplasticity reveals the brain can change and may well be one of the most extraordinary discoveries of the twentieth century.[12]

Studies now show that children aren't always stuck with the mental abilities they are born with. Indeed, the damaged brain can often reorganize itself so that when one part fails, another can step in. If brain cells die, they can at times be replaced. Many "circuits," and even basic reflexes, that we think are hardwired are not.

In my own estimation, this doesn't mean that all illnesses can be cured, but they can be treated. This provides optimism for early detection, intervention, diagnosis, and treatment with a variety of therapeutic interventions that may include counselling, pharmaceuticals, etc.

This aside, why are only one of five children receiving the mental health services they need? Might it be that we dismiss the signs of mental illness as "normal, typical teen behaviour" as they go through puberty? Puberty—from the perspective of an insect, to pupate—is to morph from one state to another. That's why many parents excuse changes in their teens' behaviour. We need to have a better understanding of what normal pubescent behaviour is, and it isn't.

As parents, we are warned about teens and their raging hormones, which we're told will lead to mood swings, acting out, lethargy, and single-mindedness for the things they love. We know that the brain isn't fully developed until the age of twenty-one, leaving youth vulnerable with limited problem-solving skills and an inability to see beyond the moment. Sometimes it can be challenging for adults to understand how difficult children's problems are, because we look at their problems through adult eyes. That which seems unimportant to us may be overwhelming to young people.

We have pride and want to protect ourselves and our children. We may want to avoid labelling them, fearing that the label could create more harm than the behaviour, so we run the risk of overreacting or under-responding

---

12 Norman Doidge, *The Brain that Changes Itself: Stories of Personal Triumph from the Frontiers of Brain Science* (New York, NY: Viking, 2010), xviii–xix.

to our children's concerns. For example, some of you may be able to relate to labelling a teen's lethargy as laziness. Or you may write off anxiety as merely overthinking things, and we may dismiss hyperactivity can simply call it being dramatic.

My point is this: at what point do we take a good hard look and listen to our own intuition, which is telling us that something isn't right? At what point do we take an inventory of the frequency, duration, or intensity of these symptoms and observe just how much they are interfering with our children's ability to cope with the daily tasks of life?

Our greatest challenge as parents is to remain present with our children throughout all of life's circumstances, including periods of confusion, chaos, and ambiguity. At times this will require us to rein in our own worries and concerns and instill hope in our youth's ability to cope.

Having said that, it is not our job to diagnose our kids. Rather, our job is to support them in getting the help they need.

According to psychoanalyst Erik Erikson's theories of human development on identity and the life cycle, we know that youth ages twelve to eighteen are all about discovering their identity; the scope of their world is their peers, and they long for fidelity. In a day and age of advanced technology, with more influences, standards, and pressures than previous generations ever had to face, it's no wonder our teens are confused and depressed.

With the world at our fingertips, who doesn't get anxious and overwhelmed? Back in the day, managing ten to twenty friendships would have been a stress all on its own, not to mention the stress of dealing with family. Today, kids are connected to hundreds of friends through social media, and they no doubt experience a glimpse of the pressures facing Hollywood stars to be all things to all people. Our kids are bombarded with choices, distractions, and curriculums that are introduced at ever earlier ages.

Let's not forget that kids don't necessarily have the maturity to process all that they're exposed to. The end result may well be tech-savvy citizens, but are we taking the time to help them be emotionally intelligent and learn to navigate their own emotions, let alone develop empathy for someone else's? The statistics suggest we are not, as approximately five percent of male youth and twelve percent of female youth, ages twelve to nineteen, have experienced a major depressive disorder.

As a therapist, thirty percent of my clientele come to me for help dealing with issues of anxiety and depression. I share these stats not to scare, but to educate about the prevalence and reality of mental illness. There is no doubt that the process of maturing will be turbulent, so we shouldn't be alarmed by the varying degrees of flux a person may experience before their mental health becomes a mental illness that needs to be treated.

Unfortunately, there are no straight answers. A diagnosis begins with a healthy dose of intuition on our part, coupled with trial and error. This is not to say that diagnostic tools and treatments don't exist, but in and of themselves they are not an exact science.

In their book *Beyond Crazy*, Julia Nunes and Scott Simmie write,

> If people are noticing some substantial changes in a child's behaviour… something is going on. It may be depression. It may be something else. But there is no harm in getting it checked out… It is a checkup like any other checkup.[13]

In *If Your Child is Bipolar*, authors Cindy Singer and Sheryl Gurrentz dialogue about the similarities and differences between raising a child with bipolar disorder and raising a child who is neurotypical. They speak to the fact that raising a bipolar child affects every aspect of your life as well as your child's. Since bipolar disorder causes behavioural symptoms, many parents experience a kind of pervasive hypervigilance when their children are doing well and when they aren't.

The authors acknowledge that having a diagnosis and a team of medical supports doesn't magically make things better. However, it does allow parents to attribute their children's negative behaviours to their brains' chemical imbalance. In many cases, this recognition also helps parents stop beating themselves up for bad parenting—or worse, assuming they have a bad child. In sickness or in health, it is a reality that your child's disorder will continue to be a major focus in your life.

---

13 Nunes and Simmie, *Beyond Crazy*, 157.

The following is a list of some activities that you have to do in addition to running a home, working, "typical" parenting, and having a personal life. If anyone wonders why you're so busy and tired, share this list with him or her:

+ Dispensing medication
+ Going to doctor's appointments
+ Going to the pharmacy
+ Expending tremendous amounts of energy trying to get your child to accomplish basic tasks of daily life, such as brushing teeth and getting dressed
+ Meeting with or talking to school teachers and counsellors
+ Observing your child's behavior and helping her avoid spiraling
+ Maintaining a mood log
+ Maintaining a medication log
+ Supervising your child when she's with siblings
+ Supervising your child when she's with friends
+ Taking your child to get blood tests
+ Submitting claims to the insurance company
+ Dealing with the insurance company
+ Doing the daily chores that a typical child would handle independently, such as cleaning his room and making his bed
+ Deciding how to appropriately respond to misbehaviour in order to provide a learning lesson to avoid a rage
+ Going to therapy appointments for yourself to help handle stress and keep perspective
+ Getting up in the middle of the night to check on your child or be with him or her if she's awake
+ Rearranging your schedule to take your child's mood into consideration (e.g. rescheduling a

haircut or play date if she's raging at the time you're supposed to go)

+ Implementing behavior modification techniques, such as reward charts or point systems
+ Reading parenting books
+ Researching bipolar disorder
+ Watching for effects and side effects of medication
+ Worrying about your child, your effectiveness as a parent, the decisions that you're making, the effects of the medications on your child's body, etc.
+ Hoping and fearing for the future[14]

One thing that can be especially challenging with raising bipolar siblings is observing their emotional teeter-totter without being on it, and wanting to control their emotional ups and downs. I'm not their regulator, but I can function as a moderator, helping to point out early warning signs of a possible manic or depressive episode. I can encourage prevention rather than be reactive to a crisis. Sometimes both the prevention and reactive roles are necessary, because even the best interventions aren't guaranteed to stop the ugly beast when it rears its ugly head. Even when you think you have your child all figured out, new symptoms will pop up. The only constant, as the saying goes, is change.

When my children don't receive my observations well, I can use my voice at a psychiatric appointment and share my thoughts, perceptions, and concerns. Chances are that teens will listen when your concerns are validated and reinforced by professionals. Although you can never force treatment, you can strongly advocate for it and spell out the consequences if their recommendations are not adhered to.

When parenting children with disabilities, it's also important to recognize the needs of your child/children who don't wrestle with these struggles. They often end up in caregiving roles and take on additional

---

14 Cindy Singer and Sheryl Gurrentz, *If Your Child Is Bipolar: The Parent-to-Parent Guide to Living with and Loving a Bipolar Child* (Los Angeles, CA: Perspective Publishing, 2004), 97–99.

responsibilities to "be good and help out." It is essential to notice when this happens, appreciate their efforts, and take the time to celebrate their own successes and challenges. Carve out one-on-one time with them when possible, and remember that it's not the quantity of time that matters, but rather the quality of time. Grab a Tim Hortons treat, watch a movie together, or have them initiate an activity of their own choice.

Don't forget to offer both formal and informal supports to these children, whether they appear to need them or not. Their needs may not be as obvious as those of your other children, but they are equally important. Allow time to vent, cry, scream, and grieve if necessary. Every child is unique.

Also don't be surprised by your change in roles when parenting children with disabilities. In a twenty-year span, I went from being a full-time homemaker to full-time student to full-time therapist, and now I'm a full-time nurse, case manager, pharmacist, writer, and professional public speaker. Being a parent of a disabled child demands different things of us at different times. Each is essential and needs to be exercised with caution to avoid burnout.

Free

Let your hair down, run into the golden fields,
twirl in circles as the sun lights up your hair.
Laugh, smile, hug the air. Take it in and be free.

—Josée Leclair

21.

SELF-CARE:
BUILDING
ENDURANCE
FOR THE
LONG HAUL

Melody

ALTHOUGH THERE ARE MANY COMMONALITIES BETWEEN THE experiences of different caregivers who raise children with mental or physical illnesses, there are also many distinctions. It's important to recognize the uniqueness of each and every situation. No two situations are alike, even when there is a common diagnosis. When you've met one child with bipolar disorder, you have merely met one child with bipolar disorder.

In today's day and age, the number of children with disabilities is on the rise, largely because of advances in technology that have improved the life expectancy of people who previously may not have survived.

As many as twenty-five percent of people may need to care for someone with a disability at some point in their lives. In 2012, eight million Canadians (twenty-eight percent of the population aged fifteen and over) provided care to family members or friends with a long-term health condition, disability, or problems associated with aging.[15] These stats are daunting, and they underline the reality that you may very well face these challenges in your lifetime.

Raising a family can be stressful even without having to support someone with special needs, which can be an isolating journey and have a profound impact on a family. Caregiving is a complex and demanding role.

---

15 "Family Caregiving: What Are the Consequences?" *Statistics Canada*. November 27, 2015 (https://www150.statcan.gc.ca/n1/pub/75-006-x/2013001/article/11858-eng.htm).

Clinical observation and research reveals that assuming a caregiving role can be stressful for both the patient and the caregiver.

Caregiving has all the features of a chronic stress experience, including physical and psychological strain over long periods of time, accompanied by high levels of unpredictability and uncontrollability. It also has the potential to create secondary stress at work, on finances, and in relationships. Most parents don't anticipate having to take on this role and are therefore ill-prepared for it, having few or no supports in place. At the time of a child's diagnosis, parents and families often experience a period of crisis and shock, culminating in an ambiguous grief, all while attempting to navigate systems and acquire available supports.

Self-care, simply defined, is our ability to care for the body, mind, and soul. So what makes it so easy to say and so hard to do? Some people may say that self-care is selfish, or that they would do it if they just had more time. They may offer a multitude of other reasons to justify allowing themselves to run on empty. Our society almost applauds a person's ability to do more and more in less and less time, yet these people increasingly find themselves in doctors' offices, counselling offices, or the ER, looking for solutions to ailments, hoping for a quick fix.

Do we consider the result of such self-neglect? Are we paying attention to the early warning signs of potential compassion fatigue (burnout) or depression? Have you ever considered the fact there's an indisputable correlation between our mental and physical health, and further, that there is a correlation between how we take care of ourselves and how capable we are of taking care of others?

Mark 12:29 says that we are to love others *as* ourselves, not more than ourselves. We can't give what we don't have. Meeting the needs of both the caregiver and the care recipient fosters joy and energy rather than depletion and frustration.

Using the principles of banking as a metaphor, think of self-care as debits and withdrawals. If the bank statement says you've got no money, you've got no money. Sure, you may have credit, but it comes with a cost. Banking and caregiving both require careful budgeting to balance the bottom line. In the same way, ignoring your basic needs can cost you, and you'll run the risk of becoming overwhelmed, exhausted, and resentful.

So how do we safeguard against these risks? For starters, self-care and self-love go hand in hand. As caregivers, it's important to adopt an attitude of healthy altruism rather than one of total sacrifice. It has been said that charity starts at home. Therefore, giving to others begins with giving to yourself, which is an act of love.

No matter the circumstances, the wellbeing of the child is inextricably linked to the wellbeing of the caregiver. I cannot stress enough the importance of your own personal health as the caregiver. Stress begets stress and calm begets calm. Take care of yourself.

Caring for a family member with a disability can wear out even the strongest of caregivers. Work hard to maintain your personal interests, hobbies, and friendships. Don't let caregiving consume your entire life. Be vigilant about your own needs and the needs of other family members, as well as your child with special needs.

An Instilled Thought of Love

One by one, sticking a note of love, building up
in my head, creating a thought up definition, all
I know is what is said—love is foreign to me.
What you tell me and show me—I will take
your word for it. What if I were to love simply
because I was told I was in love. That could be
the case. I believe I loved him. Love has volumes.
It is what is instilled. What you gather. Your
feelings individualized by only you, no one else.

—Josée Leclair

22. MY TRIBE, A TRIBUTE

Melody

FRIENDS PLAY AN INTEGRAL PART IN ALL ASPECTS OF LIFE. IT HAS BEEN said that friendship isn't about who you've known the longest, it's about who has walked into your life and said "I'm here for you," and proved it.

Our natural inclination is often to push the people in our lives away during times of crisis. Our desire to appear strong and self-sufficient can outweigh our need for help, often to our detriment. My prayer is that you will find the courage and strength to instead allow these people to come near, to walk alongside you, to share your burden, carry you when you cannot take another step, and pray for you when you have no words to pray yourself.

Here are some of the ways my friends have been there for me.

April. April is a spiritual director who attends the same church we do. During one of my biweekly visits with Pastor Debra, she asked if I would be open to meeting a woman who was in a similar situation for potential friendship and support.

At first I declined. My immediate thought was, *Too risky. What if she is as needy as I am—or worse yet, even needier?* However, after some weeks, I had a change of heart. It softened when my husband returned home from a men's prayer meeting where he had met April's husband, heard about the situation involving their son, and nudged me to get in touch. I figured I had nothing to lose.

Upon our first meeting, we clicked. It was so refreshing to be with someone who just got the complexity of mental illness, as well as the chronic stress and ongoing caregiving that's required. We each shared our journeys, detailing the good, the bad, and the ugly.

After our initial visit, we committed to being intentional friends, and we now meet weekly to share, vent, and encourage one another. It was equally refreshing to realize that someone else could work in the same field as me and have a life as complicated as mine.

Know that you are not alone. Find people in your court to rally with you!

Tracey. Tracey and I have been friends for more than ten years. We have raised our kids side by side, attended the same church, and more or less done life together. Tracey and I are friends, and so are our husbands and our children. She is and has been a teacher, mentor, and genuine friend.

We originally met through our eldest girls, who at the time attended the only French school in Guelph. I have fond memories of day trips, Bible studies, play groups, and coffee times I spent with her. We even took a trip to the East Coast. Perhaps oddly, I have vivid memories of eating crepes elbow to elbow with a group of women crowded into her tiny kitchen.

Early on in our friendship, Tracey felt the need to inform me of her mental illness; she had bipolar disorder. At the time, I knew very little about the disorder, only that the mother of another good friend of mine also had it. We briefly discussed what it was and how it impacted her, and proceeded to be friends without a second thought.

Over the years, we have maintained our friendship through thick and thin, through sickness and in health. We have seen each other at our best and worst, and up until my kids developed their own mental illnesses, a lot of what I knew and have learned about bipolar disorder is due to her. In fact, when I was completing my master's degree in Spiritual Care and Psychotherapy, I did a case study on her and convinced her to make a slideshow of her life story. I earned a ninety-five percent grade on that project and still owe her bigtime for her willingness and courageous vulnerability.

I have always admired Tracey for her loyalty, dedication to health and wellness, tenacity, and quest for joy. She really shatters the stigma of mental illness for me, and I know that our tribe of friends would say the same. She has always been an inspiration. I feel assured that my kids will lead fulfilling lives because I have seen Tracey do the same. She is a wonderful mother, wife, and friend. Now she is not only a teacher, mentor, and friend to me, but also to Luke and Josée. She offers them hope, consultation, and a compassionate ear.

Serge also appreciates Tracey's husband Guy, who from time to time initiates texts in Serge's mother tongue, asking, *As-tu le gout d'une bonne bière?* Translation: Do you want to go for a good beer?

I believe this is a man's way of reaching out to a brother in need.

Kerri-Ann. Kerri-Ann and I have known each other since we were teenagers. We originally met and were introduced as co-counsellors named Chipper and Elmo at Hidden Acres Mennonite Camp. Who would have thought those childhood careers would follow us into adulthood?

Kerri-Ann went on to earn her Masters in Social Work and works as a counsellor. Our shared experiences in life, through joys and loss, have solidified our friendship. Kerri-Ann was the first friend I went to when I got pregnant out of wedlock at the tender age of twenty-two. She lovingly encouraged me to tell an adult and suggested her mom, which I did. They supported me in telling my family and have stood by my side ever since, and for that I am forever grateful.

There are so many other ways in which we relate to each other, but some of them are Kerri-Ann's stories to share, and others are my secrets to bear. I cherish all the times we've spent making Christmas concoctions for family and friends, and summer salsa fiestas. We may not always be efficient, but we are organized.

Amanda. Amanda and I have known each other for more than ten years. Our paths crossed through church and multiple Bible studies. I sometimes wondered if she scouted me out to be her friend by signing up for the same groups, so alas I had no choice. Ha!

Anyway, when we met she had a home daycare and I recall the many playdates and visits we spent together with squealing and snotty-nosed kids. The Vaseline on her carpets never fazed her in the least. Her hospitality continues to be outstanding.

My favourite memories include her trip to visit us in Montreal, which involved a shopping spree and makeover that left one of us laughing in our seat. I also recall the time we decided to make salsa and had no idea how many jars five bushels of tomatoes would make. Boy, were we up to our elbows in tomato juice! One thing I've learned about Amanda is that she doesn't do anything half-ass. Go big or go home is her motto. We chopped tomatoes for what seemed like two days straight until the job was done. Amanda—know that I have permanently etched into our original recipe how many jars of salsa five bushels of tomatoes make. Way too many!

I will be forever grateful for the time she met me at the hospital when Josée was in crisis, and then had the foresight to think of my children who remained alone at home. I also thank her for the cooler full of meals she provided to help us get on our feet again. Amanda truly wears her heart on her sleeve, and I am privileged and honoured to have her as my friend.

Jan. Gotta love Jan, is what I say. She came into my life at just the right time. Although we haven't known each other for long, it has been a good time and I look forward to a lifetime of love, laughter, and spa days. We originally met through a church plant that we later unplanted and left.

Her joie de vivre is absolutely contagious, and she can rally a group of friends together and pull off events like nobody else I know. She is wild at heart and has a tender spot, too. It isn't often seen, but those who know you know you well can see it. I thank her for the times she has opened up, and for the countless times she's shown up on my doorstep to go for walks, drop off a meal, visit my kids in the hospital, pamper me, or take me away.

Linda. My twisted sister. The day Linda fell and hit her head on the ice was an accidental trial, but a mercy in disguise—for me anyway. I joked that God must have known I needed an angel to help us in our time of need. Perhaps he had intended to bring Linda to her knees and went a little too far? Well, who can know the mind of God?

She and I met through church, made an instant connection, and I hooked her and her hubby up with our tribe. The rest is history.

Our Mennonite heritage bonds us, not to mention journeying through the mental health systems for our children—and, as of late, for ourselves. I treasure all our car rides to and from various hospital visits and doctor's appointments, our long chats, and illegal backyard fires, even if the June bugs drive some of our friends away.

I am forever grateful that Linda adopted our middle child and took her in as her own. I knew our friendship would last forever when she didn't hate us after her battle to bring Karina to Belize.

Bonnie. Bonnie is a friend and neighbour. She is so thoughtful and kind, always checking in on me and watching out for my best interests. We walk together, talk together, and share what I have now come to call "healing tea." I love the fact that she lives a stone's throw away and is willing to be called on day or night—okay, within reason.

I hope she knows that I appreciate her willingness to talk about anything and hang out with me on a good or bad hair day. I'll always remember when she hugged me in the lane after Luke went into crisis and I began to fall apart. She helped pick up the broken pieces of my life and make something beautiful out of it.

Also noteworthy: Bonnie is a local artisan and makes bohemian creations from materials found, thrifted, and recycled.

My tribe: Tracey, Jan, me, Linda, and Amanda.
Credit: Laura Drost.

Unfolded Beauty

Beauty defines the lines in her face, beauty is
the fireworks of green in her eyes, beauty is the
tear she sheds for every lost smile, beauty is the
personality that comes out when she talks, it is
beauty lost when you don't know you have it,
beauty is what's translated when you speak fire
with your eyes, beauty is traced from the inside
out, beauty is defined within, what you reveal is
true beauty.

—Josée Leclair

23. FRIENDS AND FAMILY PERSPECTIVES

Amanda

OUR FAMILIES HAVE BEEN FRIENDS FOR YEARS. WE HAVE CAMPED together and had many dinner parties. Our kids have had sleepovers, and they go to each other's birthday parties. We celebrate life events and holidays together and help each other out when we're having a bad day. Even though we're not blood-related, we are family. We ask each other to be emergency contacts for our kids at school.

In short, before the diagnoses of sick kids, we already had a solid foundation to our friendship.

I remember getting the phone call. Melody was obviously overwhelmed and upset, and all she asked was that I meet her at the ER because Serge was out of town. Josée wasn't well.

I went and stayed with Melody, sitting with her as we waited for the doctor to come. What do you say? How do you help a friend when you yourself are scared, unsure of what's going on and wondering what to do to help? All I really could do was be present, be there, and pray.

The next day, I felt so helpless. I didn't know how to "fix the problem," or what to say or what to do. So I did what I knew: I cooked. I brought over enough meals to feed them for a week. In fact, they were probably sick of my food before they got through it all. But I felt that I needed to do something tangible.

It's hard seeing your friends struggle. It's hard when you can't relate to the situation. I haven't had to deal with mental illness with my children, so how could I help a friend going through it? What could I offer?

I struggled with the guilt of not having issues with my kids in health, behaviour, or education. If the Christian cliché is true, that God only gives you what you can handle, then God must think I can't handle much—and that Melody can handle a lot! I've come to hate that cliché. I think God gives people more than they can handle, but then he puts others in their lives to help us on the journey.

I needed a calm family life to be able to walk with Melody during this period. Life is a journey, and we sometimes walk the path on our own. And sometimes we walk it with others.

Melody and I are part of a group of women who regularly get together. Our common faith has helped us. We also love cooking, enjoy good wine and cheese, and often engage in heart-to-heart talks.

For years we have done an annual girls weekend without kids or husbands, as well as a mother/daughter weekend. As the mom of a sick child, Melody needs to take care of herself, too, although that isn't her first thought. On a few occasions, we've had to make her take care of herself when she didn't do it for herself. Talking about how things are going at home is important, but it's also important talking about other, less important things, to share funny stories and get away from the everyday stresses.

When we found out that Luke was sick, that he was in the hospital but not yet diagnosed, we all had a very difficult time. How could this possibly be happening to two of her kids? Hadn't their family been through enough? How could we help? Again, I defaulted to making meals and praying.

I remember calling Linda, another mom in our core group of friends, and asking her what I should do. She gave the best advice: "You can't get them out of the hole they're in. They're in deep with no obvious way out. All we can do is jump in and be in the hole with them." As a group, that's what we tried to do. Listen. Hug. Pray. Cry. Have a girls night.

I tended to text every few days to touch base. "Hey, how is your day? I am thinking of you." I felt it was less intrusive than a phone call, in case she didn't want to talk. But I was still letting her know I was thinking of them. We also went out for lunches, had cups of tea, and just spent time listening.

When Luke was hospitalized, but was starting to do better, he was able to come home for a weekend. Melody called and asked if my kids could come over. My first reaction? Panic! How would my kids process seeing Luke on medication, talking slower, or acting different? What if they said something inappropriate? Goodness knows how many times I loosely use the terms "I'm going crazy" or "She's nuts" or "I will lose my mind if…" How often as a society do we use those phrases without thinking? What would my kids do if they didn't know what to say?

I agreed to get the kids together, as I knew it would be good for Luke to be with his friends. On the car ride over, I chatted with my kids. I explained a little of what I knew, and what I thought they should expect.

I don't know why I was panicking; the kids played well, enjoyed being together, and when Luke started getting tired we left. After all, kids can see how parents react. If we show our friends love, support, care, and empathy, they will learn those skills, too.

I have witnessed my good friends be amazing parents. I've learned so much about grace and dignity from them. I've seen unconditional love displayed, as well as fierce love and protection. Those kids are lucky to have been born into a family with parents who are willing and able to provide them with the support they need.

What have I learned from all of this? That it's okay to not know what to say. It's okay to be scared. It's okay to help out in a way that you're suited for, such as cooking meals. For others it could be driving to appointments, taking care of pets, other kids, or household stuff, or even helping out financially. I've learned that it's okay to say, "I have no idea what to say or do. Can you tell me what you need?"

I have learned that letting them know that you care, that you're thinking of them, and that you support them is important. Even if that's all you can do, it's way better than silence. I've learned that it's okay to ask questions. Parents quickly become experts, so listen and learn. I've learned that no two journeys are the same, so giving advice and anecdotes about what worked for someone else isn't always helpful.

In short, I've learned that there is no "normal." And besides, normal is overrated.

Matthew

I didn't know what I was seeing.

I still don't know what was going on that afternoon, but I now know that it was significant.

Sitting across from me in a downtown café, Luke was bouncing ideas off me—he was building a talk on mental health, opening up his heart and mind to me, his youth pastor.

"People are more than a label," he said. "Don't make jokes about mental illness. It isn't funny. People struggling with their mental health need respect and understanding."

In hindsight, there were cues that something deeper was going on—the times of vagueness in conversation, the superpowered optimism. I just thought that he was overexcited, and Luke chocked it up to a cold he was getting over.

On this day, I cut the meeting a bit shorter than I had planned. Luke's thoughts were getting unclear, and it looked like he had reached a limit.

The next day, Luke was in the hospital.

I will never forget when Luke saw me next. He was at the far end of a long hallway at the Parkwood Institute. With a huge smile, he came running and gave me a hug. He was glad that I had come.

But I was struggling with the whole situation. Would I make things worse? What should I say? What was the protocol here?

It was a bittersweet visit. I'm still so very grateful that I got to see Luke, but it was like someone had pressed the pause button. Luke wasn't fully Luke. Or at least, he wasn't Luke as I remembered him, as I expected him to be. His spark and passion was restrained. His animated talking was replaced by slow and careful speech. He felt faraway and yet close. Luke was there, but he also was not.

We chatted through the strategies he was given to regulate his mood, Luke's dream to see Iceland, the T-shirt from his grandparents he was wearing, how much he loved chicken teriyaki subs, and how hard it was for him to be there. He wanted to get out, but I couldn't get him out.

I couldn't fix Luke.

I couldn't make it better.

The only thing I could do was be there, and I believe that made all the difference.

Tracey

Melody and I have known each other for over ten years. She has been there in some of my darkest hours and also some of my best. I admire her quiet and reserved personality. She does so much for everyone while remaining cool and collected. I knew her profession of being a counsellor was the right path for her, as she is a great listener and has fabulous advice to offer. Such a great friend.

I watched all her children grow up, and that's why, when I heard that Josée was bipolar, I just couldn't believe it. It seemed too hard to comprehend what had happened. I was completely dumbfounded. I had been diagnosed bipolar when I was thirty-one. I knew the many doctor visits that were to come, the many med changes that would be necessary, and the time it would take for her to feel "normal" again. Don't get me wrong— once you figure out how to manage it, it isn't that bad, but getting there can take years. Second-guessing every emotion you have and wondering if you're *too* happy or *too* sad can be challenging.

I went to see Josée in the hospital and kept thinking that the doctors were wrong.

She's fine, I thought. *It's just a little blip.*

However, over time, my opinion changed. It was hard to see another human unstable from being bipolar, as it made me wonder if I had been like that. I knew my husband Guy had been through a lot when I was diagnosed, but had I caused the grief in him that I now saw in my friends? Melody was so quiet. I knew she was processing things. I found it hard to relate to her. I don't know what it's like to have my child diagnosed.

I couldn't fathom the grief she was going through, and yet I wanted to help. I decided that the only way I could help was to talk to Josée and tell her that she would be whole again. I listened to her and provided feedback where I could.

For my friend, I decided to enlist my husband. Guy could relate to how Melody and Serge were feeling. We would all get together to talk. Guy and I would listen and then offer feedback. Guy felt it was important for them to know that they must take complete control over Josée's life. Monitor her comings and goings and her drugs. We both felt that a quiet atmosphere would help her heal, as it had for me. We also talked about the many medications and their side effects. I let them know that some of them made one feel numb and out of it, while others weren't as potent.

Josée's diagnosis brought back many painful memories for me. Seeing her and seeing my friends deal with it was surreal. It had taken me eight years to get my life back after my diagnosis. Eight years during which friends and family had stuck by me, and now I was seeing just what that meant from another angle.

And yet I felt so useless. Even with my experience to pass along, I felt that I wasn't helpful. You see, through this time I learned that no two bipolar diagnoses are the same. We are all individuals, and therefore so are our diagnoses.

Guy and I had preached tranquillity to Melody and Serge, and yet they surrounded themselves with many family and friend visits. They took Josée camping and to get-togethers. And we learned that this was all good for Josée. She benefitted from the support, whereas too much stimulation for me had made me anxious and depressed, as I couldn't follow all the conversations.

With time, Josée found her new normal. She was great at talking about it, and I always thought she was so good at articulating her feelings. A good quality, given her diagnosis.

I admired how the Leclair family openly discussed the disorder and their family's struggles. It brought so much more support their way, which was beautiful to see. But they didn't just talk about it... they researched it. Serge and Melody read books, looked up articles online, and got as much information from the doctors as they could. In time they started to teach me instead of the other way around.

When Luke was diagnosed, it was another shock to the family—and another surprise to me. I know there had been talk of Luke's diagnosis beforehand, but to hear he'd had a psychotic break was sad news. I could tell that this was hard on Melody and Serge. In particular, Melody seemed to get thrown back into grief, but deeper this time. They travelled to the hospital almost daily and I can only imagine how exhausting that must have been. I didn't worry about them as much this time. I knew they knew what to do.

Luke was also working hard at getting better. He seemed to soak in everything that was taught to him. He could also articulate what he was feeling very well. I believe this helped the doctors assist him. I think it's a testament to this family, how well they can articulate things. It's something I struggle with, so I admire this quality.

As I write this, I think the family is still working on their new normal. I feel like Melody is getting better and isn't sitting on the edge as much waiting for the next bomb to drop. Serge and Melody have done a wonderful job of guiding their children to assess themselves and help to determine the right path for their care. I think this helps them to become independent.

I'm looking forward to many more years of doing life with this family and watching their children grow up to become even more wonderful than they already are!

Winston (aka Grandpa Martin)

At fourteen years of age, our oldest granddaughter, Josée, was doing some babysitting for a neighbour. At the end of her day, she quickly grabbed her bike and took off at full speed. She stopped at her teacher's house, exhausted. Immediately the teacher saw her strange behaviour and called Melody, suggesting that Josée be taken to hospital. Melody was shocked, but very quickly followed the teacher's instruction and took Josée straight to the Guelph hospital.

After hours of the admission process, with lots of questioning and repeating of interviews by different hospital personnel, it was finally decided that Josée, who was in a manic state, should be transferred to the psychiatric unit in Grand River in Kitchener. Her mother wasn't allowed to accompany her, and it was a very traumatic experience for Melody to see her daughter being taken away from her. Serge was far from home on a job, travelling as fast as he could to get home.

Eventually Josée was diagnosed with bipolar disorder and spent several weeks at the hospital, being put on the proper medication through trial and error. As her grandpa, and a man in my seventies, I wasn't familiar with such a diagnosis, even though I had been a pastor for almost forty years. So this called us to new ways of praying and supporting the family. There were lots of questions, the main one being: how had this happened?

Eventually, with ongoing doctor visits and med changes, Josée stabilized and has had only occasional setbacks.

Then, after about five years, something similar happened to her younger brother. Luke, at fifteen years of age, had come to our home in Stratford for the first weekend in February 2017. All seemed to be fine, as he was his usual pleasant, talkative, intelligent self. He returned home, and by Monday morning things changed rapidly. We were shocked to hear of his behaviour. He was also sent to the Grand River psychiatric unit and eventually diagnosed with bipolar disorder, in addition to his previous ADHD condition.

What was happening to this family? It has changed our lives, too, to learn a lot of new information and rely on more daily prayers for healing and wisdom.

Luke's experience was prolonged. After three weeks at Grand River, he went to Parkwood in London for another six weeks. This was a whole new experience for all of us. The hospital was a wonderful modern facility where Luke was confined and observed, and he learned many new coping skills there. He knew that he needed to be there. I was amazed at the program itself, as it was very personal and helpful. He enjoyed his supervisor, fellow patients, and the staff, and he was a friend to all.

In visiting Luke, we had several occasions to avail ourselves of the hospitality provided by The Ronald McDonald House, only a few blocks from the hospital. While his family stayed there, they were able to avail themselves of various resources to help in understanding what was happening, all of which was helpful for Melody in her counselling job.

The Leclair family has been sharing their experiences with different groups interested in mental health. Their truthfulness about dealing with life's curveballs will hopefully help others to seek out the necessary help. Their push is sometimes needed to get the right services to respond.

Their family has grown closer together through this experience and they have felt the support of God, the church family, friends, and extended family.

Betty Ann (Grandma Martin)

The first weekend of February 2017, Luke came to our home in Stratford to spend some time with his grandparents before the beginning of his next semester of Grade Ten. We've always enjoyed special times together and this was no exception. However, we weren't prepared for the events that were to unfold.

On Tuesday evening, Melody called, explaining with a soft voice what was developing on the home front. Monday, the first day of Luke's new semester, hadn't gone well, but we passed it off knowing that Luke finds any change in routine difficult.

By Tuesday evening, Luke was exhibiting unusual patterns of behaviour and seemed to be rapidly "changing channels" with many different mood swings. Melody asked if we had noticed anything unusual on the weekend. The only thing we could think of was that he had visited his cousin one evening and talked nonstop on the topic of ADHD—a topic he wanted to share with his youth group to help them understand the condition he personally dealt with on a daily basis.

When his cousin left, he had wanted to continue explaining it to us, his grandparents. His story seemed quite repetitious and lengthy and left us struggling to understand just what he was trying to say. It was getting past his 10:00 p.m. bedtime and I did wonder how he would settle down to sleep for the night.

The following morning, everything seemed fine.

The next thing we knew, Luke was being transferred from the hospital in Guelph to the psychiatric unit in Kitchener, where he stayed for three weeks before being transferred to Parkwood in London. He was in a manic state and thought he had been struck by lightning at the time of his admission.

We had some knowledge about the services offered at Grand River, since Luke's oldest sister had previously been a patient there. At first, we were in shock and prayed hard for Luke, his parents and siblings, and for the doctors and nurses who would be assessing him. It was sad to learn about that his bipolar diagnosis. How could two siblings from one family be affected so traumatically? How would their parents be able to cope?

Realizing how important it is to pray and trust that God is present and ready to help each step of the way, we alerted Melody's siblings and asked for prayer. Later we shared with our church family and asked them to join us in prayer. This helped to ease the burden while questions and uncertainty remained.

We were unable to see Luke for ten days as he was basically confined to his room, unable to sleep on his own or cope with visitors. His dad was able to snap a photo of him standing at his "therapy wall" and email it to us. It was such a relief just to see him and hear about his ever so slight improvements. How could such a normal-looking young man have such big problems looming inside him?

It was soon evident that Melody and Serge had a good group of supporters. Serge began to write emails note to inform Luke's supporters of his progress. Sharing in this way was good therapy and gave specific prayer requests. It's safe to say that Serge felt God's presence and support through his friends as he dealt with the burdens and questions accompanying this illness.

We were so proud of both Melody and Serge as they struggled to balance the needs of Luke and their two daughters while also looking after home and work affairs during those troubling days. Even through discouragement and tears, they pursued their desire to educate others by sharing their experiences in an attempt to help remove the stigma surrounding mental health.

Drawing on much strength from the Lord, Melody and her two daughters honoured a pre-booked appointment to join a group of ladies for a special annual breakfast to share about their personal journey with Josée, now nineteen years old, who had been diagnosed as bipolar five years earlier. They didn't include what was happening with Luke, as his illness was still being diagnosed at the time.

Melody also took time off work as a counsellor to work through the family's difficulties and make her family a priority. This kind of illness affects the whole family. She used her spare time to write down her thoughts, as therapy for herself. It later occurred to her that recording them into a book could provide help to other struggling families.

While Luke was at Parkwood, we got our first introduction to The Ronald McDonald House. What a blessing that place is for families with young children in nearby hospitals, often with life-threatening illnesses. We highly recommend it. In fact, my Quilt Club was recently in the process of making a total of fourteen Canada-themed quilts to help Ronald McDonald Houses across Canada. What a joy it was for our group to contribute!

I never once thought that I would make a personal visit to The Ronald McDonald House. At the beginning of Luke's time in London, however, he was given some passes to leave the hospital for a few hours at a time. His parents were able to stay at the House and bring Luke over for as long as he was able to tolerate. He could go to their room to rest as necessary, and he always had his "anxiety box," with tools to help him cope. His first choice of activity was to have a provided snack, then dabble in other forms of recreation. Extended family could also visit and the children could participate in crafts, watch movies, exercise, read books, and play games while Luke rested.

At times, no pass was given and family was allowed to visit at Parkwood. The visiting areas were surrounded by large glass windows, always in view of staff members. We felt secure knowing that help was available if needed. For Luke, though, being constantly observed wasn't always desired.

The institute had teachers to help patients with schoolwork they were missing. Other group activities included going outside for walks, playing games, spending time in the gym, and working on painting, arts, and crafts. These helped Luke pass the time in constructive ways.

Luke enjoyed receiving cards and visits and was especially impressed when his own school teacher and youth pastor came to visit. He needed to be connected to the community outside the hospital. He also enjoyed receiving cards from his school friends, which helped him to know that his classmates were missing him. Luke also got some telephone privileges, which helped keep him connected to family. In interacting with other residents, and seeing many different illnesses, he grew to appreciate the care his own family has given him.

Getting the right medication and adjusting to being back home and rejoining the school environment are carefully worked out with the support of family, the school, and local doctors and counsellors. The first three months home are so critical for maintaining healthiness.

Luke has need of many coping skills to keep him on course. Mental illness doesn't entirely disappear, but must be worked on throughout his life. There will be times when he is doing well and other times when some assistance is needed.

As grandparents, we love Luke and pray that his needs will be met as he journeys through the challenges of life. We support and encourage both him and his family as they bear the bulk of the responsibility of having not one but two children with mental health challenges. We are confident that God supplies the strength to carry us through when we look to him for help and guidance.

Jan

Thirteen years ago, I stood by a friend as her toddler died. Jack died of an infection that his parents didn't even know he had. Out of nowhere. And as the little white coffin was lowered into the ground, and the masses of white balloons released into the sky, and as the little toy dump trucks full of flowers was left on his grave, his parents grieved and mourned. His parents said goodbye and tried to figure out how to continue life without Jack.

This is the physical death of a child. It is awful and painful, but final. Parents say goodbye.

I can't help but draw a parallel between the physical loss of a child and the loss of the version of a child you once knew. I have only known the Leclair family for a few years, and I wasn't around when Josée had her first episode with mental illness, but I was certainly around for repeated episodes and the startling episode with Luke this winter.

During crisis, there is no time to grieve. There is no time to process what happened and what caused it, and no time to ask what could have been done to prevent it. There is the sheer mechanics of moving from one appointment to the next and trying to juggle family needs, physical needs, and the needs of the child in crisis without creating a new crisis of your own.

There is no grieving period. No mourning. No goodbye to the child who existed prior to the disease.

Right now, Josée and Luke are both home. They are stable. And now the grieving and mourning begins. The grieving of mental health, predictable schedules, stress-free family holidays, and carefree innocence. Now they must grieve the way the disease has affected the entire family, circle of friends, and even people's careers. They must grieve each time their child feels the pains of adolescence and they don't know if this will set them off. They must grieve the day they were able to wake up and not think about what state of mental health their child would be in today. The must grieve the day when they didn't feel like they were constantly walking on eggshells in their own home.

There is grief. There is mourning. There is loss. Even amongst those who are still living amongst us.

Linda

This isn't my first attempt at putting my thoughts down on paper. When Melody asked for her friends' input, I thought, *No problem. I can do that.* But that clearly isn't the case. My desire was to write down all my thoughts and feelings, to tie them up in a neat little bow. As though this is now all behind us. It's not like that at all. There are just too many layers!

Melody and Serge were the first friends my husband Ben and I made when we moved to Guelph almost thirteen years ago. Our kids grew up together. We bonded over similar parenting woes, and we share very similar views. I fact, I recall asking Melody to take our kids and raise them in the event something should happen to Ben and me! That speaks to how close we have felt to Melody and Serge.

When Josée was in the hospital and first diagnosed, I will never forget feeling the distance between us in an acute sense. Our friend Amanda called me while we were in South Dakota on vacation. I wanted desperately to hop on a plane, come home, cook meals, and spend time with Melody and the family, doing whatever was needed. A few days later, I was home cooking up a storm, eager to do something, anything to help. Listening to Melody's story broke my heart. I hoped and prayed that the right medication would be found. I longed for their lives to return to normal. Ha! What is normal? Does anyone know?

The moment I found out about Luke's hospitalization will be forever etched in my memory. I was in absolute disbelief. Shock. Denial. It couldn't possibly have happened again!

Looking back now, I realize how different my reaction was to the news the second time. My first question to Serge was, "Where is Melody, and who's with her?" Someone needed to be there for her, but I also knew that person shouldn't be me—and not because of my own injury, which happened the same day. My instinct was to keep a safe distance. What was I going to do or say? "It's going to be all right"? Shallow! "God doesn't give us more than we can handle"? Clearly not true. "Everything happens for a reason"? Zero compassion! I had *nothing* to offer. What good would my own tears be? But that's all I had.

Though Josée was only in hospital a short time, the aftermath was unbelievable. The struggle lasted long after the diagnosis. The impact of seeing a child diagnosed with bipolar disorder was far greater than I could ever have imagined. Melody was watching and assessing constantly. The dynamics in the family shifted dramatically. She had to cope with a lot of ups and downs.

Ever so slowly, though, the family adjusted. Melody had great supports in place, and she advocated for herself and the rest of her family. I thought maybe, just maybe, things would get better than she had ever hoped for.

Then February 8 happened. As a family, we just didn't know what to do. We prayed, which went something like this: "God, bring Luke out of psychosis." Two weeks later, they tried a new drug, because nothing else had worked. "God, move mountains and shake the earth beneath them!" Luke developed huge side effects from the drug. "God, do the impossible—heal him!" They planned to move Luke to London for longer-term admission. "God, don't you care about this family? How much more can they take?" We found out Luke would be in London for at least a month.

The word *helplessness* best describes the emotions we felt. We couldn't fix it. There was no ointment for the hurt, or advice on how to deal with it. Wasn't wisdom supposed to come from experience?

I prayed for Luke. I prayed for stability for Josée. I prayed for Karina, caught in the middle of an impossible situation. I prayed for Melody and Serge's marriage. Lesser difficulties had broken strong bonds.

Whatever practical help we provided felt small and completely insignificant in the big picture. Is there always a light at the end of the tunnel? What is the purpose of great suffering? This crisis hadn't happened to me, but at times I felt like I had been punched in the stomach. When would the nightmare end? No professional, educational, or personal experience can equip you to walk a journey or road that has never been travelled.

But allow me to share what I see now in Melody. A pastor once said, "Tough times don't make or break you… they reveal you." Character! It defines you. It's what people see. And here's what I see in Melody, and I know others see.

Selflessness. She set her career, her own needs aside—and it wasn't just a job to her. It had been her dream, her passion, who she had been created to be. Without hesitation, she set it aside, not knowing if or when she would be able to return. She hadn't chosen this, but she accepted it.

Vulnerability. No one likes to be vulnerable, showing their weaknesses to others. But there is an intense beauty that comes from putting down our defences and allowing others to see and feel our pain. We are all broken, but when someone opens that place of hurt it creates a sense of connection. As helpless as I felt, Melody created a space for me to enter into the grief with her.

Patient endurance. I'm sure she felt anything but patient! I recall a conversation I had with Melody around the time when Josée was meeting a new doctor for which Melody had held high hopes. Afterwards, she told me that what this journey was really about: telling and retelling her story. Stories changes here and there as time passes and new territory is covered. Melody has shown immense grace, compassion, poise, dignity, and strength in living out her story. She had a resolve to keep going, her head held high, and that hugely impacts those around her.

Joy. I'm not just talking about happiness, but joy! Through all of this, Melody has never lost her ability to laugh and have fun. She never turns down an opportunity to get together with friends. Even in the darkest moments, she greets visitors with a smile. A phone call from a nurse in London once made us both roar in laughter… Luke was refusing to shower! She looked at me and said, "That's their problem, not mine. Good luck with that!" I think in that moment I was slightly jealous.

Some days were bad and others were worse, yet she never played the victim. She got out of bed every day, put her best self on, and moved forward. Wow.

Love. John 15:13 says, "*Greater love has no one than this: to lay down one's life for one's friends.*" In Melody's case, she lay down her life for her family. She has given of herself more than she had to give—and then squeezed out whatever was left. And sometimes she's had to give tough love, too. I pray that she will be filled to overflowing with love from God the Father and from her friends and family!

Peace. Despite her circumstances, there has always been a sense of peace about Melody. Maybe that comes from having hope—hope that God will in some way redeem this intensely difficult valley she's been in. I believe that God never wastes our hurts. He can and will do incredible things through the Leclair family. Only he knows how many lives have already been made better because of their journey, and the way they share their story with others.

I have a sort of Hall of Fame in my own life—a collection of people who have had a significant impact on me. People for whom I have the most respect. People who I would do well to emulate. People I hold in the highest esteem. My Hall of Fame only has a handful of people in it, and what these people all have in common is that they have all walked incredibly difficult journeys, valleys so deep that few people could come away from them more beautiful than they were before. These people were made stronger, more compassionate, kinder, more loving, humbler, and gentler in spirit and a deeper faith—more radiant!

These people make me want to be with them. I want to learn from them and listen to their stories over and over, because I don't want to forget the many ways in which they have touched my life. They have a resilience that is rarely seen. They have wisdom that comes from a life of trusting the life-giver when everything around them has crumbled.

Melody is one of these people to me. Right before she receives that crown of righteousness, she will hear the Master say, "Well done, good and faithful servant. Come and share your Master's happiness!"

Secrets Scrawled Across Her Face

Easily misinterpreted by a fault
The truth is hidden in her irises.

—Josée Leclair

24. RECOLLECTIONS AND LIVED EXPERIENCES

Luke

THE NIGHT JOSÉE WAS HAVING HER FIRST EPISODE, WE HAD A FAMILY meeting in the living room, without Josée, in which my mom and dad explained that they would be taking her to the hospital to get help. Up until that point, we had all been experiencing a different side of Josée, one we had never seen. At least I felt assured that I wasn't the only one who felt that way.

Fast-forward to the next few days. My parents spent many days going back and forth to the hospital. They were very protective of Karina and me and kept us from seeing Josée because she wasn't herself. I recall one car ride with my Josée that parents let me go on. Josée believed she could predict the songs being played on the radio, and she sang along at an obnoxious volume. She was in her own world and very much inadequate to engage in any kind of conversation. She was being very sassy and let the music control her emotions.

I remember wondering whether or not my sister would ever be the same again. This made me feel lost.

The next thing I remember is her being discharged and our family going on a camping trip. This camping trip was very different from previous ones due to the fact that we all had to accommodate Josée—it felt like we were walking on eggshells with everything we said to her. She was very sensitive and attached to her own ideas, and she took personal any disagreement or difference of opinion. Then she would flip into euphoric episodes during which she was overjoyed with the sight of an animal in nature or having taken the perfect photograph, in her opinion.

It was becoming our new normal to have to accommodate Josée and her moodiness. Christmases were interesting because stimulant management is very important to the illness. During the first year of her illness, she went hypomanic and I remember thinking, *Here we go again.*

Our relationship was getting more and more complicated. Josée became both easy-going and irritable. It's a strange combination. It became a predictable pattern of looking good on the outside to all and then falling apart on the inside at the end of the day. A coping mechanism for the family was to have meetings together and vent about our experiences without Josée. At times we had no choice but to laugh about how ridiculous she was being. I found this to be extremely helpful. Oddly, these meetings are some of my favourite family memories.

Throughout these experiences, I have learned to focus and try to understand what Josée was going through. I've had to change my mindset and create in myself a person who, when around Josée, can look and separate the disorder from who she is. There is a lot of work transitioning between wellness and bouts of illness, and it impacts the whole family. We all struggle with expectations and knowing when or if to ask her about what caused her mood change, what triggered her responses. At times, she doesn't know.

When she's sick, she is very in the moment and doesn't respond to things in an emotionally calculated way. Sometimes our family has to go in what we call "family protection mode" and control who she sees, what she says, and follow up with folks to make sure they understand what they've just seen or heard. It can be very exhausting to keep having to see her when she's sick, because every time we think we've mastered these tools, the face of her illness changes.

That being said, there are tools we have picked up along the way that work, such a s having family conversations during or after episodes, limiting sibling interactions, and trying not to be reactive to her. When these methods fail, I hit the eject button and go visit my grandparents.

I never accepted the notion that I had bipolar disorder, even though I took a low dose of medication as prevention. I did this for over a year and a half before I raised a concern, and under the supervision of my psychiatrist and the reluctant blessing of my parents we lowered my medication in hopes of weaning off of it.

Within three days, I started getting sick.[16] I was very excited the first day of my second semester of Grade Ten. I remember the day going by very quickly, and the whole time it was very hard to focus. I was just going from one class to another like the world was spinning. I don't mean that it was a high feeling; it was more like a weird foggy feeling in my brain, like I was there and also not there, like things were happening and I was just along with for ride. Surreal. Numb.

After school, I started to question what was going on—not within myself, because I felt quite secure, but with everyone else. I started to analyze everyone and everything and came to no satisfying answers. I wasn't thinking clearly, so my questions and answers made no sense to anyone but me. My sleep was out of whack, too, but I felt that I could function as well as ever.

During this time, I was adamant about working on a mental health talk I was preparing to give about ADHD, with my youth pastor. Pastor Matt and I met to discuss the content. That night, once my mind got hooked on something, it wouldn't let go. I wrote out theories of everything for most of the night. I remember seeing the time pass quickly and tried to lay my head down to rest. I had a broken sleep.

Suddenly, I woke up and felt pain in my head. Logic led me to conclude that I must have hit my head on the wall. Then, for whatever reason, I darted upstairs. Come to think of it, in my mind's eye, I thought I saw wires sitting in front of my basement bedroom window. As I climbed to the top of the stairs, I saw a blue flicker of light that lit up the entire main floor of the house. I felt a surge of energy. Inside, I was really scared.

I went to the front door and stepped outside. First I saw wind swirling and howling, and then I saw a hydro pole crack, with two pieces

---

16 Disclaimer: just because my meds were being lowered, it's not an exact correlation. It could be a coincidence that mania followed.

breaking off. One hit the trailer we had on our yard and landed in the basement window; the other one smashed into the neighbour's roof.

Out of complete shock, I ran up to tell my mom what had happened. I yelled, telling her that I had been hit by lightning.

Keep in mind that when you're out of your right mind, things don't always happen in a chronological order. I remember my mom being in as much shock as me. We immediately went downstairs, and I took her onto the front porch to share my concerns. Believe it or not, I asked her to take me to the hospital. As we left out the back door, I pointed at another perceived broken hydro pole. My mother was more interested in getting me to the hospital. Looking back, my mom was very good at not triggering me and making me get defensive and trying to prove my point.

When we arrived at the hospital, we had to steer around some renovations that were underway. I was very cautious and scared about the potential of getting struck by lightning again—or worse, that my mother would get hit. I grabbed my mother's hand and we quickly got to the ER. My mother brought all of my scribblings along as proof that I was losing my mind.

Before long, I was put into isolation. It was clear to everyone but me that my story didn't check out. Go figure. This didn't change my conviction in any way, shape, or form. Interestingly, no staff member ever said to me that I hadn't been struck by lightning.

I was given food, drink, and blankets to keep me comfortable. The nurses kept telling me to drink water to cool my body temperature and rest so that I could recover. I would come in and out of sleeps and do doodles while being assessed by various medical staff.

Before I knew it, I was transferred to CAIP for intensive treatment. I had no idea why. The last thing I remember about the ER is being taken away on a stretcher.

At Grand River CAIP, I was taken to my new room while my parents met with staff and completed paperwork. Nurses kept me busy with colouring pages and meals. That night, I peed the bed twice. This wore on the nurse's patience and she said, "You're fifteen. You shouldn't be peeing the bed at this age." I felt really hurt by that, because I couldn't help it.

143

I was terrified and hearing and seeing things and coming in and out of manic states. It appals me that a nurse would have said that while working in a mental hospital.

I have vague recollections of this time—puzzles and other conversations with nurses kept me occupied.

Throughout this period, meds were being trialled. The first med I was put on was an antipsychotic and sleeping med, a drug my sister had once been on. However, it did nothing to help my psychosis or my sleep.

After eight days, according to my parents, I was worse off than I had been originally. So my psychiatrist prescribed a drug he thought would help. That didn't go well, either, as I had an extreme allergic reaction. I took the meds as per usual, and the next thing I knew I was eating my supper and putting down my tray because I'd started to feel weak. I fell asleep in my clothes, on top of my covers. I woke the next day and immediately started feeling really stiff all over. I assumed it was still the same day and thought I should finish my milk. Unbeknownst to me, it had been sitting out all night and had spoiled. When I tried to drink it, though, my jaw was stiff more than anything—and when I realized it was chunky, I couldn't close my mouth to stop drinking, nor could I take the carton away from my mouth; I was too focussed on trying to figure out what was wrong with my mouth.

I walked to the nurse's station as fast as I could—which ironically was slow—where I was informed that I had slept for thirteen hours. Keep in mind this was the longest I had slept in a long time. My slurred speech and excessive drooling spoke for itself, and the nurses immediately knew the culprit—the medication—and named its side effects. I awoke again around 1:00 pm and was given a different drug to help ward off the side effects. Eventually, I could somewhat speak again.

I made my way over to have supper with the other kids. I was really embarrassed because I was drooling all over my food and I couldn't chew. I had to eat soft food, which wasn't hard to find in the hospital. I could only imagine how my parents must have felt seeing me in that state.

The worst wasn't over yet. I woke up the next day with a hand tremor. When I tried to grab a glass of water, it spilled everywhere. My hands were shaking uncontrollably. I went to the in-hospital school that day and couldn't write. I felt stupid because I use my hands every day to do simple tasks without thinking about it. Suddenly it took concentration to do the most menial of tasks.

At this point I was scared that I would never get better and would always have this hand tremor. These effects took months to wear off entirely.

One and a half weeks into treatment, I began to integrate with the other patients and get involved in programs. The staff set up a plan where I would hang out with the other kids for one hour the first day, then two hours the next day, etc. Earning privileges is a built-in part of how they roll in the psych ward.

I was always paranoid that the staff was trying to test me and figure stuff out about me and push me to my limits. They kept switching my room, and they had cameras in them which made my paranoia even worse. I thought one nurse was stealing my socks.

Eventually the nurses allowed me to have full days with the other kids, and at this point I was assigned a new nurse named Matt. One morning he brought me a radio and told me just to listen to the words of the songs; if I didn't like something, I could turn it off and focus on my emotions. I felt a lot better afterwards. This helped to slow down my racing thoughts.

Every now and then, Matt would check in on me and we would chat or go throw a basketball in the courtyard—a break from the constant assessing.

One time I asked if he could have lunch with me in the courtyard. There, I told him all about the things I had made in tech class and about my other interests. For once I felt as if this was my actual life. Up until this point, I hadn't known what was going on. I finally felt like this was real. After that, Matt and I would joke together, shoot hoops, and play pass or whatever.

Around this time, I started hearing about how the other patients were sometimes issued passes to get out of the hospital. I wanted this for myself, so I talked to my psychiatrist the next day and she informed me of the process. It started with monitored phone calls only to my parents, and then progressed to in-hospital passes where I literally could go up to the next floor. This allowed me to see my sisters for the first time since I'd entered the hospital. We grabbed subs and played Uno.

Until this point, I stayed connected with friends and family via letters which helped sustain me and made me feel loved. I read them over and over again. I found it very grounding. It got me out of my head and helped me to connect with what was actually going on. The most memorable card was given to me by my best friends, the TeNyenhuis family. It was homemade, and it had a disc on it, symbolic of my friend Kyle and I playing disc golf. The card said, "I saw the disc getting bigger and bigger—and then it hit me." When I opened the card, it had a pop-up bouquet of flowers. On the other side of those flowers was a monster, meaning that all my monsters were actually flowers. My friend Alden also wrote something in the card, along with a joke that made me laugh.

On occasion my grandparents came, and I eventually worked up to out-of-hospital passes, which progressed to home passes. For my first home pass, we bought chips and pop and I had all my friends over. I really appreciated how eager my friends were to see me even though I wasn't well.

Twenty-one days into treatment, I was told by my psychiatrist that CAIP was a temporary place and that I had a choice of whether or not to go to a longer-term facility for continued care. I figured things could only get better. Once again, I followed hospital policy and had an ambulance transfer me in a stretcher. The ambulance attendants were nice, and I was looking forward to being in the Parkwood Institute.

When I arrived, I was greeted by Kiel, the child and youth worker there. He was friendly and asked me where I was coming from. He got me food to eat and gave me a tour of the place. I was especially excited to see the room with a radio and calming wall. There were also snack rooms where you could bring your own snacks and eat at your leisure. The Parkwood Institute had a courtyard, too, and a fresh air room with pockets in the wall that allowed air in.

At the time, all the patients were about to come in for a community meeting, so I got to meet them. Needless to say, it was a very mixed crowd with varying degrees of need. I should also mention that I was the only guy. In general, more girls check in for long-term care than guys. I think it has to do with the fact that some guys just aren't as open to treatment.

I started in-hospital school the next day. In truth, I really didn't have the attention span for it and didn't want to go, but I pushed myself anyway.

That day, I met with my new psychiatrist along with my parents. I was informed about treatment and programming, and I gave my consent. We created a six-week treatment plan. I remember thinking that six weeks sounded like a long time, considering that I alrady thought I was back to being healthy. I felt upset and very confused.

I also had to restart the pass system. It seemed so unfair that I had to start from scratch. After all, my illness was the problem, not me, and yet we were both being punished.

It was hard to understand where to draw the line. You have to be responsible for your actions while at the same time realizing that you're not always in the right frame of mind to make wise choices. I was caught up in my emotional mind and had to closely monitor my stimuli in all regards: light, sound, touch, etc. At times my parents had to threaten to leave their visits early if I found them to be too triggering. This was particularly upsetting, as I didn't always have control. However, I understand from their perspective that it must have been really difficult for them to see me like that.

Once I had gotten to know the other patients, I could see their true colours. Some of them were really mean. I quickly learned who I could talk to and be with, and who I couldn't. I also continued going to school at the hospital and worked on modified workloads that were manageable.

I saw my psychiatrist every couple of days and eventually worked myself up to weekend passes. At this point, I realized that I had hit a second swing with my mania, which settled down after I was prescribed a new medication. It still took time for my healing and recovery to begin. I recognized that I wasn't always thinking straight, but I appreciated my family's visits just the same. I felt as though every day was one big dream during which nothing happened in chronological order or made sense. I was too busy in the trance of the dream to judge my thoughts.

I eventually got around to the last two weeks of my stay, and after a home visit I cried that I had to return to the hospital. All my friendships there were forced, whether I liked it or not, because we had to do activities every day like community meetings, bowling, art therapy, music therapy, and cooking. During March break, we went on an outing to the mall and theatre. We also had therapy group with dialectical behaviour therapy, as well as going to the gym and courtyard.

The only person I genuinely liked and got along with was my Kiel.

When discharge day came, I was finally free, so to speak. The next few weeks were all about reintegration meetings during which my parents and I met with the school principal and social worker to create a safety plan, complete course selection, and discuss my credit situation.

I was very anxious to get back to school, but I was concerned about meeting my classmates. What would they think of me? Would they be wondering where I'd been? In the end, there was only one student who bothered me about it, and I proceeded to obtain all four of my credits in a two-month timespan, which I'm thankful for. All my teachers were very proud of me.

Life has since returned to my new normal. I have lots of support and am future-oriented. I like to concentrate on my abilities and my future rather than dwell on how my life will never be the same again and the meaning of it all. Apart from taking meds, seeing a psychiatrist, getting blood work, and receiving counselling, life is good.

I'm forever grateful to have been born into a family who is understanding and helps rather than pushes me out. Without their support, I would not be where I am today.

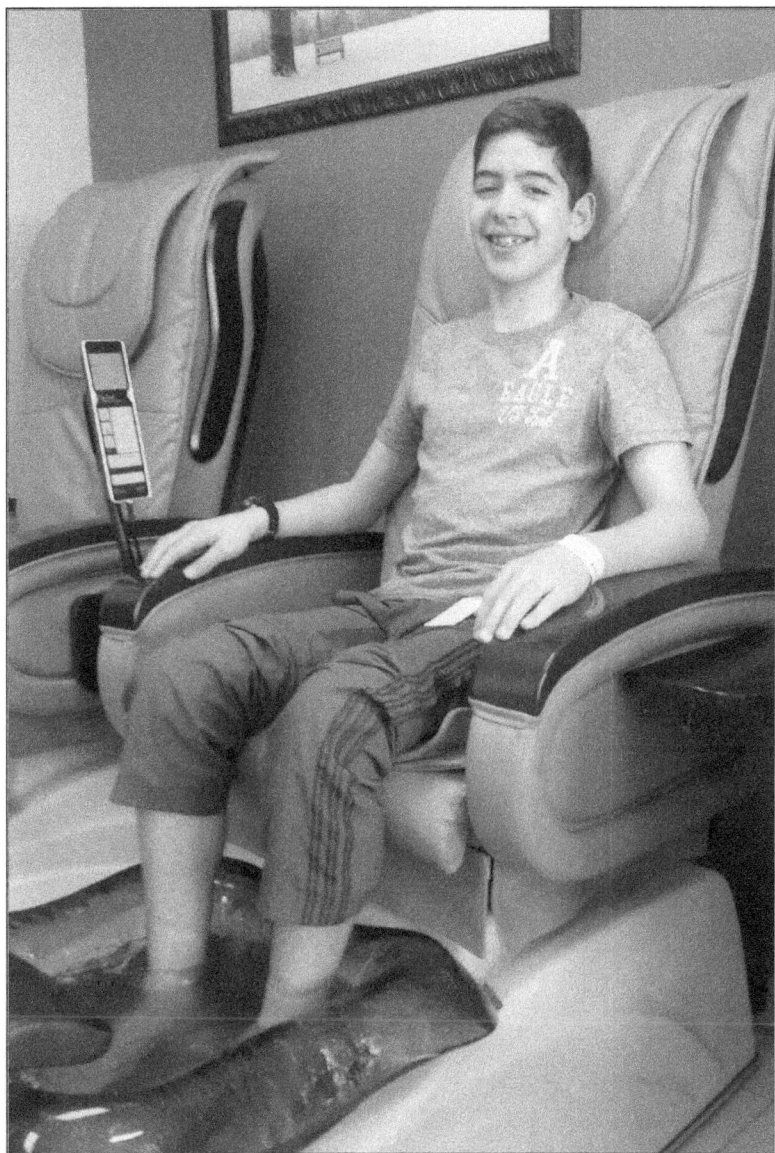

Luke getting a pedicure while on a hospital pass.

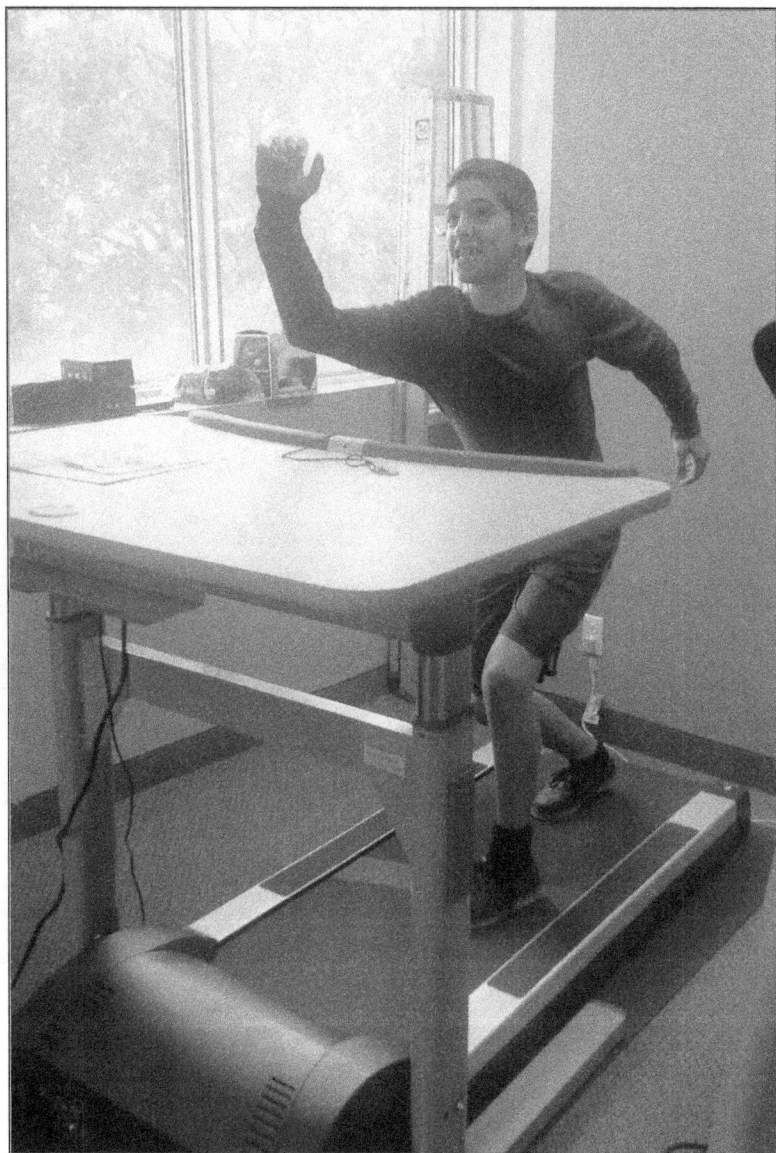

Luke at a psychiatry appointment running off his steam.

One of the many precious cards Luke received from friends while in hospital.

What's Up Luke

You are AWESOME and that will never ever change! No matter what you are not defined by your circumstances, like what you are going through now, you're defined by your personality! Luke you will always be brilliant, hilarious, a good good friend, a light when people walk into the room, dedicated, compassionate, and one of my bestest friends. I want you to know that I've been praying and thinking of you. I am not worried Luke because I know that you are stronger than whatever you are facing. Keep on rocking life Luke and know that these things remain,

+ God loves you!
+ All of your family, friends love and care about you!
+ And you are incredible!

From: Amber Bamber

Time	Day 1-2	Monday	Tuesday
7-7:45	Wake-up/breakfast	Wake-up/breakfast	Wake-up/breakfast
8:00		Let's get moving	Let's get moving
8:30	Initial assessment with Psychiatry	Personal hygiene/ self-care	Personal hygiene/ self-care
9:00	Nursing check-in	School skills building/ check-in	School skills building/ check-in
10:10	Break	Break	Break
10:30	School skills building	School skills building Crisis/safety planning/ academic work	School skills building Crisis/safety planning/ academic work
12:00	Lunch/social time	Lunch/social time	Lunch/social time
12:30	Room time	Room time	Room time
1:00	Introduce Smart goals	School skills building Time management/ stress tolerance	School skills building Time management/ stress tolerance
2:00	Group	Self-care skills building Spiritual care w/ Nursing & CYW	Self-care skills building Coping skills w/ CYW & SW
3:00	Individual time with Nsg. support	Individual time with Nsg. support	Individual time with Nsg. support
4:00	Recreation activity	Recreation activity	Recreation activity
4:45	Dinner/social time	Dinner/social time	Dinner/social time
5:30	Pass/visitor prep	Pass/visitor prep/ homework	Pass/visitor prep/ homework
6:00-8:30	Home skills building Visitors/off-unit passes	Home skills building Visitors/off-unit passes Room time 6:45-7	Home skills building Visitors/off-unit passes Room time 6:45-7
8:30	Quiet time/review day with staff	Return from pass/unit chores/Media-based learning	Return from pass/unit chores/Media-based learning
9:00	Relaxation/sleep skills	Relaxation/sleep skills	Relaxation/sleep skills

An example of day programs available in CAIP's psychiatric ward.

Time	Wednesday	Thursday	Friday
7-7:45	Wake-up/breakfast	Wake-up/breakfast	Wake-up/breakfast
8:00	Let's get moving	Let's get moving	Let's get moving
8:30	Personal hygiene/ self-care	Personal hygiene/ self-care	Personal hygiene/ self-care
9:00	School skills building/ check-in	School skills building/ check-in	School skills building/ check-in
10:10	Break	Break	Break
10:30	School skills building Crisis/safety planning/ academic work	School skills building Crisis/safety planning/ academic work	School skills building Crisis/safety planning/ academic work
12:00	Lunch/social time	Lunch/social time	Lunch/social time
12:30	Room time	Room time	Room time
1:00	School skills building Time management/ stress tolerance	School skills building Time management/ stress tolerance	School skills building Time management/ stress tolerance
2:00	Self-care skills building Substance use w/ Nursing & CYW	Self-care skills building Emotions mgmt/ Mindfulness w/ CYW & SW	Self-care skills building Healthy relationships w/ Nursing & CYW
3:00	Individual time with Nsg. support	Individual time with Nsg. support	Individual time with Nsg. support
4:00	Recreation activity	Recreation activity	Recreation activity
4:45	Dinner/social time	Dinner/social time	Dinner/social time
5:30	Pass/visitor prep/ homework	Pass/visitor prep/ homework	Pass/visitor prep/ homework
6:00-8:30	Home skills building Visitors/off-unit passes Room time 6:45-7	Home skills building Visitors/off-unit passes Room time 6:45-7	Home skills building Visitors/off-unit passes Room time 6:45-7
8:30	Return from pass/unit chores/Media-based learning	Return from pass/unit chores/Media-based learning	Return from pass/unit chores/Media-based learning
9:00	Relaxation/sleep skills	Relaxation/sleep skills	Relaxation/sleep skills

An example of day programs available in CAIP's psychiatric ward.

A Thought for Yesterday and a Thought for Tomorrow

I sit on my couch and ponder
I think about yesterday and the events that took
place
Some events make me cringe while others leave
me smiling
I thought to myself they all prepared me for
today's events
What will tomorrow bring?
The possibilities are endless
I ponder all that could happen
Maybe something exciting will happen or maybe
something aggravating
But perhaps it is best to leave it in the mystery
And let each day prepare you for the next

—Josée Leclair

25. IN THE CENTRE OF BETWEEN

Karina

DURING LUKE'S HOSPITALIZATION, I REMEMBER ONE PARTICULARLY awful day. Mom had scheduled a meeting with the social worker at the hospital for Josée and me, so we could vent and ask questions. That same day, Josée had to write an entrance exam for college, but our timelines got crossed, traffic was bad, and we couldn't find parking. When we did, Mom couldn't figure out how to use the automatic parking dispenser that was evidently not so automatic. She nearly lost her marbles trying to figure out how to get the receipt after providing payment. Clearly her nerves were shot. At that time, the smallest of things could cause her to fall apart.

We ended up being late for our appointment, and Mom and I left Josée at the college without telling her that we'd even had an appointment, since she was still writing her exam and we couldn't reach her.

At the hospital, my mom went to see Luke briefly, and we bumped into Grandma and Grandpa, who were there visiting him. That further delayed my return to school. When we got back, Josée was upset because she had missed the appointment and later found out she had failed the exam.

When we finally got back to Guelph after a very long day, I made it to school just in time for the last five minutes of third period. I saw my friend Clara and spewed out my account of the day through blubbering and tears. Clara didn't say a word. She just gave me a hug.

I felt mad and in shock, wondering how this could be happening to our family again. I was in denial, since I had no idea how to deal with it.

Fortunately, I was able to process things a little better because it was the second time around. Through seeing my parents struggle with the crisis, I learned that they are human, too. Like all people, parents cry and make mistakes. We tend to think our parents are perfect. But even when my parents were at their worst, they maintained themselves, each other, and our family.

Ben and Linda are really good family friends, and in fact I consider them to be a second family; we joke that I am their adopted daughter. Ben is a teacher and last semester, with my permission, he told one of his co-workers, who now works at my school, about my situation and asked him to reach out to me. Mr. Pollari did just that, and I went to him alongside my friend Gillian for a talk.

I told him everything that was going on. It wasn't just Luke's crisis that was all-consuming; many of my friends were going through different things. My best friend's father had just passed away from a massive heart attack. After I'd filled Mr. Pollari in on everything that was going on in my life, he encouraged me and assured me that I would be okay. He reminded me that while it seemed like everything is falling apart, eventually it would come together. He shared personal experiences that helped to give me perspective. He is also a Christian and was able to encourage me in my faith.

My friend Gillian was a big support for me during this time. She went to see Mr. Pollari with me every time I went. She was always there for me when I needed her to be. In fact, all of my friends were a huge support, checking in and asking how things were going. They were always there for me and giving hugs when needed.

Youth group was another big support for me during this time, specifically Angela, my youth leader, and my best friend Lauren. After youth group, the three of us would talk and share what was going on in our lives and support one another. Angela had been my youth leader since I was twelve years old and always initiated get-togethers outside of our weekly Bible studies. Whether it be for ice cream, breakfast, or dinner, she would pick us up and drive us home. She made time for us even though she had to attend full-time school and had piles of homework. And for that, I am forever grateful.

Two big escapes during this time of crisis were rock-climbing and my part-time job at Meltwich, a local restaurant. Rock-climbing provided me with an outlet to get let go of my anger and convert it into positive energy. It allowed me to be in the moment and not worry about the next thing. Meltwich was another great outlet. Josée's ex-boyfriend, Josh, who knew precisely what was going on, constantly checked in with me there to ask how my family and I were doing. There was no awkwardness between us. We were just buddies. Going to work also got me out of the house and away from what most days felt like a zoo.

This time around, I felt signs of depression more intensely. I was unmotivated to go to school, and when I was at school I would shut others out and avoid talking about what was on my mind. Although my friends were there for me, they were busy and had their own lives to deal with. I was in a lull during this very low period. When I told Mr. Pollari, he normalized my ups and downs, assuring me that my experience was different than Josée's and Luke's and reminding me that I was still accomplishing things even though I didn't feel "normal." My life eventually got better with time, patience, giving myself credit, and talking about it.

The hospital's visitation rules were different with Luke than they had been with Josée, since Luke's experience was more severe. Josée and I couldn't visit with him until two and a half weeks in. I thought this was very unfair, since I was a biological member of the family. I thought it unfair that my parents could see him but we couldn't. I feared that Luke might mistakenly die while in hospital, and I wouldn't get to see him again.

Now I can appreciate this rule, because if we had seen him in that state it may have been harder for us than for him. When we did finally see him, he was definitely different. He wasn't himself. It was like seeing a different person, almost as if he was a grandpa version of himself. What I mean by that is that he was very slow to catch on to things. He walked funny, and he had a bit of a tremor. These symptoms eventually went away, but his personality still took some time to recover.

Towards the end of Luke's time at Parkwood and his final discharge, I went with my best friend's family to Disney World in Florida. This was a great trip that allowed me to escape from everything and relax without my family.

Although it was a fun trip, it was also difficult because my best friend's father had died just a month prior. Their family had a missing piece. The family kept it together and knew when to take breaks, and they didn't push their boundaries. Often we would split up, with my going to the parks with her brother's friend while the rest of the family hung back at the hotel. It was refreshing to see everyone have fun and let go. Overall it was a great trip. I really enjoyed myself and hold them all in my heart.

Addicted to the Act of Rebellion

A rebel heart, caught in the act, addicted to the
feeling of going against the current—the rush,
the adrenaline, the look of defiance, the fear
making you feel powerful. It is even harder to do
good. Make no mistake in breaking a rule with
intent, rules need to be broken once in a while.

—Josée Leclair

26. WHEN YOU CAN'T JUST FIX IT

Serge

FOR OUR TENTH ANNIVERSARY IN 2007, MELODY AND I PLANNED A trip to the Maritimes for two weeks. The girls went to Melody's parents and my parents came to our house to look after Luke. We had a wonderful trip, and everything went well. Upon our return, though, my dad took me aside and advised me that we should get Luke assessed and screened for behavioural issues; he was very stubborn and set in his ways, and he went from zero to sixty at the flick of a switch.

"Aw, he's just like me," I said, defensively. "There's nothing to worry about."

My dad is a man of very few words, however, and every word that comes out is premeditated. He looked at me in a very stern way, and said, "No, there is something more at play here."

That was the end of our conversation.

Days, weeks, and months passed and Melody and I went on with our lives, haunted by that conversation. Every time Luke acted up, I couldn't help but think of my father's advice. During this time, we were living in Montreal, although we were only there for a two-year work contract and we didn't bother to establish a medical team for the family.

When it came time to move back to Guelph, Melody and I decided to get our son assessed.

Throughout Luke's grade school years, he was always an easy target for bullies due to his reactivity and inability to control his responses. One of his determinations was to become good at basketball, and when Luke took on something it was all or nothing. He was very disciplined.

When it came time to try out for the eighth grade basketball team, Luke was devastated that he didn't make it. We encouraged him to ask for constructive feedback from the coach. When he did, the coach told him that he had the skills but displayed poor sportsmanship and didn't demonstrate an ability to temper his outbursts. It wasn't that his actions were mal-intended, he just had poor impulsive control.

People with bipolar disorder maintain a vivid imagination into their adult years. Not knowing this at the time, we often accused Luke of lying and distorting the truth. We know now that his perceptions were recreated in his head to the point that he actually believed them. This is why we often didn't report the bullying, because we were never really sure how much was real and how much was in his head.

Luke never had big groups of friends. He would spend all his time with just one or two people due to his perseverating nature. This became a problem in Grade Eight when his only friend, his sole lifeline and defender against the bullies, left for India for two months. The months of November and December were especially hard, and the situation was exacerbated by the fact that Luke was never very good in school, at least in conventional ways, and teachers had to accommodate him.

Melody and I went into a parent-teacher meeting to discuss what Luke was going through, and we found his main teacher to be no-nonsense. Luke had an Individual Education Plan and was on a rotation system with several teachers, which made it hard to establish these accommodations. Two of Luke's other teachers ended up joining our parent-teacher meeting to address the dilemma, but things didn't get much better. The road was paved with good intentions, yet that year still proved to be one of the most challenging years of his elementary career.

The extended Leclair family has a Christmas tradition, which is to rent a cottage for a few days over the holidays and spent the time together. It's always a big party atmosphere, and it's a priority for my mom that everybody is happy and plays by her rules—which means no rules. And as a grandparent, her grandkids can do no wrong in her eyes.

The Christmas of Luke's Grade Eight year, Melody and I gave up trying to implement bedtime curfews and monitor his sugar consumption. We would go to bed without knowing when he finally fell asleep. Luke had always had a sweet tooth, and since kids don't have the best self-control mechanisms in place yet, this was a recipe for disaster.

It all came to a head the morning we were scheduled to return home from the cabin. We had been together for four days and Luke hadn't taken care of his personal hygiene. With a three-hour car ride ahead of us, I put my foot down and told him that he had to shower. Luke and I have a tendency to go head to head; he is especially stubborn and at times his stubbornness fuels my own. After we'd had a yelling match, his grandmother came to his rescue, as usual. But that wasn't good enough and he stormed out that winter morning into snow, barefoot with no coat on. My mother thought she could coax him back in, but she was unsuccessful. All she could do was leave his boots and jacket close to the bush she saw him hiding in.

He stayed out there for what seemed like hours as I proceeded to pack the car, leaving a spot for him to sit in the back. I told the girls to go back into the cottage and say their goodbyes. During that time, I suggested that Luke would likely sneak into the car. I also told the girls not to comment on what had just happened.

When we got back to the car, as anticipated, Luke was in there, buried in the luggage.

We must have been quiet for at least an hour or two. That's when Karina said we had to talk about what had happened and deal with it. So we had a family discussion about personal boundaries and self-care and establishing these standards for oneself even when they weren't imposed.

I suspect that Luke hardly slept during those four days, and when school started the next day, it didn't go well. His friend still hadn't returned from India, and one afternoon Luke ended up at the principal's office, claiming that he was being bullied. But the principal saw the situation otherwise. During her investigation to sort out what had happened, Luke voiced his frustrations and said that sometimes he just wanted to kill himself. With that, the principal now had the duty to report the situation and classify it as suicidal ideation.

I remember the phone call. She explained to me what had transpired between Luke and this other boy. She explained that she didn't believe this was a case of bullying, even though Luke did; she felt that Luke's perceptions of the situation came across as exaggerated and distorted, and in his frustration he had voiced that he wanted to kill himself. She advised me to take him to a walk-in clinic at the Canadian Mental Health Association (CMHA), and if I committed to taking him she pledged not to pursue the case any further.

We went to CMHA the following Tuesday, the same place Josée went to see her psychiatrist since she had been diagnosed two years previous. In the meantime, Luke's paediatrician, Dr. Promnitz, referred him to see Josée's psychiatrist, Dr. Edwards, who accepted Luke because he was a high-risk case.

After Luke was assessed, Melody and I met with Dr. Edwards and she explained to us that because Josée was bipolar, Luke had a good chance of developing it—four to six times higher than normal. We were confused, though, as the warning signs in him seemed to be very different than Josée's. Dr Edwards explained that with boys, bipolar disorder often presented as episodes of increased irritability and reactivity. She felt that his clearly episodic pattern of reactivity and sensitivity suggested early signs of bipolar disorder.

However, we didn't have enough firm clinical evidence to support a diagnosis at that time. Instead he was given a presumptive diagnosis of bipolar disorder, after which we considered a few options. We opted to start treating Luke with a mild dose of a medication commonly used to treat symptoms of bipolar disorder. Our hope at the time was to keep a potential manic episode at bay since manic episodes are traumatic and we had already lived this experience with Josée.

I guess you could say the medication was working, because things calmed down for a bit. When the situation did escalate, we would increase Luke's dosage and he would calm down again. This resulted in his dosage creeping up to four times the original amount within eighteen months. By this time, Luke was in Grade Ten and still had no formal diagnosis, except for the ADHD. He was convinced that he didn't have the same illness as Josée. This resulted in a constant battle to make him take his meds.

By the fall of 2016, Luke managed to convince us that we were fighting the wrong beast. At the time, he was in a special outdoor education program that took him outside the school grounds. His sisters had each gone through the same program and had done extremely well. But for some reason, Luke was struggling; I don't know if it was because he had extremely high expectations of himself or if the lack of structure created a difficult environment for him to learn and grow in.

After consultation with Dr. Edwards, she recommended that we make the medication change at the end of the semester, so as to avoid any potential problems during Luke's exam period. We agreed, and that brought us to early 2017, the end of the first semester.

Looking back, when I recall the outbursts of anger and lack of self-esteem that prevented him from creating solid friendships, it wasn't enough to diagnose him. When it comes to bipolar disorder, the condition is greater than the sum of all its symptoms. There is a formula to a diagnosis; without going through what was about to unfold, there was no way to label his moods and behaviours with any degree of certainty. I say that because the last thing I would want for any parent is to overanalyze their kids and jump to conclusions. No medical strategy can prevent the inevitable.

Indeed, no one could have predicted the perfect storm that was about to hit.

It was the end of the semester, and because Luke's special program required no exams he was left with a week and a half of unstructured time at home. By then, Melody, Josée, and I had had the opportunity on three or four occasions to tell our story at churches and mental health events. Luke had attended one of those and seen the satisfaction it created for us and others.

Unbeknownst to us, Luke slowly started developing a desire to come up with his own talk about how he coped with mental illness—ADHD, in his case. Or as he liked to coin it, "severe ADHD," to make it sound that much more serious.

Given his perseverating nature, it came to the point where this talk was all he thought about, and during this unstructured time he didn't have anything else to distract him. This led to many sleepless nights as he ruminated over his ideas. Luke became very agitated and short-fused, driving the rest of the family up the wall. Melody and I, looking for respite, decided to send him to visit his grandparents for a couple of nights, hoping that he would calm down without his siblings present.

To our regret, when he came back he was just as amped as when he had left. Melody and I had dinner plans the night he returned, and we were no sooner out the door than we started receiving texts from Josée that Luke was in her face and scaring her. I chocked it up to sibling rivalry and directed them to spend the rest of the evening in separate quarters.

When we got home, Melody and I divided and conquered. Josée explained Luke's behaviour to Melody, saying that he would turn his head sideways in the middle of his rants and say "Got 'em." At one point, he had announced, "And now, for dramatic emphasis, I'm going to swear." And then he proceeded to swear off at her.

We managed to do some damage control and get them off to sleep— or so we thought.

The next morning brought the first day of the new semester. Luke was overly excited, as he was going to be entering level two of the machine shop class he had developed a passion for in Grade Nine. Also, I was leaving for a business trip to Montreal.

That evening, the girls and Melody could feel a storm brewing within Luke. They just didn't know what it was. A real storm was brewing, too, and the next day school was cancelled due to the risk of freezing rain. I had grown up in northeastern Ontario, where school only got cancelled when freezing rain paralyzed the city, but in the south a mere forecast was all it took.

Another day with no structure had Luke coming undone. That evening, since I wasn't home, Melody had to play taxi to get the kids to extracurricular events, and she could hear Luke talking to himself in an aggressive tone. At one point, Melody asked if he was hearing voices and he said yes.

When Melody dropped Josée off at skating, he asked to call me. It was 7:00 p.m. and I was in my hotel room. I picked up the phone and don't even remember answering before Luke started on a rant, explaining everybody else's problems, naming disorders in people that didn't even exist, and insisting that he had a solution for all of them. Somehow, in the twenty-four hours I had been gone, he had acquired his PhD in psychiatry! He was using a pressured speech that was all too familiar. After only a few minutes the phone call was over, without me getting a word in edgewise.

When he hung up, I felt that this confirmed he was bipolar. I immediately texted Melody to tell her to call me in privacy. She agreed with my thinking, but we had been down this path several times before with Josée and knew the delicacy of picking the right timing to take Luke to the hospital. Many times with Josée, we had been turned back at the ER because, even knowing her history, they felt that her symptoms weren't severe enough to admit her. This creates extra trauma at the beginning of an episode because the person with the symptoms feels as though no one is giving credibility to what they are experiencing, which leaves them alone with their demons.

So we agreed to keep a close eye on Luke until we felt there was enough evidence to head to the hospital. I remember hanging up the phone and having knots in my stomach, a very uneasy feeling. I was seven hundred kilometres away and I wanted desperately to jump in the car and come home. However, I looked out the window and saw that the storm which had been merely forecast in Guelph was lashing Montreal for real.

It made no sense for me to hit the road at 8:00 p.m. after having worked all day, so I went to bed with one ear open and the phone by my bed. Sure enough, the phone call from Melody came at 5:30 the next morning, indicating that the time had come where they would take us seriously at the hospital. After she told me what had happened in the night, I agreed with her and told her I would jump in the car and meet her at the hospital as soon as I could.

Coincidently—or Godcidently—I ran into a friend from church as I stopped at a coffee shop on my way to the hospital. Pete Kuehni had served as a Bible study leader and mentor for Melody and me. I briefly told him what was going on and he hugged me, saying he would pray for us. This gave me more fuel than my coffee could have ever have provided me.

When I arrived at the hospital, I knew just what to do.

Melody and I went our separate ways that afternoon, but when we got home later we discussed our need to take the upper hand with the system and set our emotions aside in order to advocate for Luke effectively.

For example, psychiatric wards all have a policy stating that patients are not to stay in contact with other patients they meet in hospital. The reason is that it's unhealthy for patients to develop friendship or other kinds of relationship outside hospital walls, since these relationships can sometimes exacerbate their issues. In our family's case, though, we saw no way to prevent this with Luke and Josée. We couldn't prevent, and didn't want to prevent, these siblings from having a relationship with each other. And as they were both teenagers, they obviously needed to still live in the same house.

When we visited Luke the next day, we were prepared to emphatically state that Luke would need to remain in the hospital and then get checked into a long-term facility until we could properly prepare for his homecoming. It felt counterintuitive as parents to force the hospital to keep our child, but we had followed our intuition once before with Josée, bringing her home after only eight days of treatment. We now knew that had probably been a mistake.

Thankfully, the hospital staff listened to us. By the time they got Luke stabilized, the social worker had already sent a formal request to the Parkwood Institute for admission and it had been approved.

By the time Luke arrived at Parkwood twenty-one days later, Melody had taken a sick leave from work to help support Josée, who was being exposed to the illness from a different set of eyes. She saw the anguish it created for the family and concerned friends, as well as the financial and emotional toll it took. While trying to process this, she was also dealing with school stressors and challenges, navigating boy relationships, and a rejection from her college of choice.

I asked Dr. Edwards if there were any case studies we could read on how to parent siblings with bipolar disorder. She told me that she didn't know of any. I felt confused, as two years prior she had explained that when one child has bipolar, the siblings have a heightened change of developing it. So how could it be that there were no other cases?

I asked three psychiatrists and always received the same response.

Dr. Edwards clarified that it wasn't that there were no documented cases of bipolar siblings, just none where the siblings still lived together. Apparently our kids had developed early-onset bipolar, triggered by hitting puberty. The majority of people aren't diagnosed until their twenties or beyond, at a point when they aren't usually still living under the same roof.

Sometimes in life it's good to be one of a kind. Other times, not so much.

When I look back on the lives of both Josée and Luke, I can easily identify the times when they were unwell before their diagnoses. What I don't want is for parents to overanalyze their children. A lot of what children experience may be completely normally, and probably is. On the other hand, I would still encourage parents to be vigilant and listen to others—as we eventually did in the case of my father's earlier advice.

My upbringing was very much mind over matter. If I didn't feel well, my mom would say, "Ah, it's all in your head. Just go for a walk, get some fresh air, and you'll feel better." If those things didn't work, I just had to accept it and get on with my day, kind of the way a sore throat feels awful when you first wake up but starts to feel better as time passes, even if you don't do anything.

I've had to do the same thing with my kids. Sometimes there's nothing I can do but accept that they are who they are and that the dynamics of their disorders, woven throughout their characters, make them the unique and amazing people they are. Don't get me wrong, I'm a normal father with hopes, dreams, and aspirations for my children. However, I have come to accept that they will still be able to achieve great things despite their limitations. It is in knowing their limitations and learning to self-advocate that they will be able to get there.

The summer before Luke's crisis, I had an experience while camping that exemplifies some of the emotions I've experienced while walking this road. One morning, I woke up to a very thick fog—the kind you could almost slice with a knife. Our family had a waterfront site, with the shore only fifty feet away from our tents. But I couldn't even see the water.

I thought about how cool it would be to jump into my kayak and paddle into the depth of this fog. The experience of living on the edge was empowering for me, so I jumped in. Since it was only six in the morning, my family was asleep, and off I went on my own, paddling into the abyss. Adventure or stupidity?

I kept looking behind me until the shore had completely disappeared. Then I set my paddle down in the cockpit and took a breath. For some weird reason, it felt great to be in the unknown. It was soothing to feel as though I could disappear, since that was what I craved at that moment.

When I felt that I had gone close enough to edge of danger, I turned the bow around to head back, only I didn't account for the amount of drift I'd experienced since putting down my paddle. I was much farther from shore than I had expected. Fighting back panic, I started paddling frantically.

Just when I thought the situation was hopeless, the shoreline appeared. When I reached it, I sat on the ground and slowly watched the fog that had almost swallowed me.

The grief I've experienced is like that fog; it comes on unexpectedly, there are days when I feel completely lost in it, and it can take what feels like an eternity to dissipate. I have to remind myself often that the grief will take time to lift, but when the sun does break through the fog it always heralds a beautiful day.

Unrelenting

Change, something that is consistent, we as
humans like predictability, but we need change
and change needs us, it is the minute that turns
on the clock, it is the space drawn out between
play of events, it is the vibration that is made in
your mind when you keep walking and seconds
pass, when you keep walking and minutes slip
under you, hours creep up the walls, days sneak
up behind you and you're teleported into weeks,
months come to scare you, before you know
it another year has gone by leaving only the
remnant of memories, disguised in the passing
time. Is Change hiding its face, silently making
revolutions behind your back? Somehow change
has its way of creating a better future than you
could ever make up yourself.

—Josée Leclair

27. WHEN NOTHING IS THE SAME

Melody

MONTHS AFTER LUKE'S DIAGNOSIS AND CONTINUED TREATMENT, I came upon my own personal storm. I wasn't coping well with the uncertainty of it all. I wrestled with this, not knowing which parts of my experience accounted for me grief, loss, trauma, anxiety, and depression. This was especially hard since my husband and I weren't coping the same way.

Fatigue set in and I felt lost, alone, as though I had been given a life I never asked for yet had no choice but to carry on living.

My kids and husband depended on me, but I fully recognized that I had nothing left to give. I felt as though I had somehow lost all my empathy. What a terrifying thought that is, since empathy is the marker of my work as a therapist. It felt selfish to admit it, but I could only muster enough empathy to get myself by. It was like I was an elastic band that had gotten stretched so far that it had snapped. How do you stay resilient when you've lost your elasticity?

After months of contemplation and self-judgment, I finally swallowed my pride and admitted to my doctor that I needed pharmaceutical support. My emotional reactions had exceeded my capacity to cope with them. I was over-overwhelmed, if you will. With respect to the prospect of taking medication, I remember thinking, *If I cannot beat my kids—figuratively speaking, of course—then I may as well join them.*

Nothing was the same. Family getaways and camping trips now required an immense amount of planning. Packing used to be about food and clothing, but now it often included safety planning and medication maintenance, as well as making sure backups are in place in case of emergency. For Josée and Luke, a bad night's sleep wasn't a just a bad night's sleep. It could result in drastic mood swings—or worse, manic episodes.

I grieve the small stuff. How things used to be. Camping and being off the grid. Encountering the adventure of the unknown. Eating when you're hungry and sleeping when you're tired. Since the onset of my kids' diagnoses, leaving our routines behind means putting their emotional stability at risk. It's hard to understand why this is so. All I know is that routines grant them the comfort and safety they need.

This is not to say that we stay home all the time and completely cater to their legitimate needs. Rather, we have to negotiate outings wisely based on what's going on with them. As the kids age, they can take more responsibility for themselves. Still, at times we have to do things differently for the success of all.

Words to Me

I want to bring meaning to words people didn't
know had meaning, each word I use drips in
my experience, something no one else can speak
to, words mean far more than perceived, it is
personal, it is raw, it helps you let go, it helps you
move on, they make a statement, I believe my
words to mean purity, words depict emotion,
written word defines past, present, future, it is
our time capsule, I believe everyone can write,
everyone has a word, and that word may cure
many souls, it is the word the next person is
looking for, writing is a voice, it is consistent,
it has no apologies, it tells the truth, writing is
more to me than a paper and a pen.

—Josée Leclair

28. LIVED EXPERIENCES, LEARNINGS, AND POETRY

Josée

IT'S HARD TO REMEMBER WHAT LIFE WAS LIKE BEFORE IT. WHEN I WAS twelve or thirteen, I was just a girl who either felt too much or not at all. I knew a neighbourhood girl who had struggled with her moods, too, and I was aware that she had bipolar disorder. I had little understanding of what that actually meant. All I knew were the usual stereotypes of rapidly changing moods without control. Little did I know that it's not as erratic as that. My twelve-year-old self, who'd had some exposure to the disorder, had no idea what she was in for.

In my fifteenth year, I felt robbed—whether I was manic, depressed, or in the hospital, there was no time to simply be fifteen. I was a deer in headlights. By September of my Grade Nine year, I felt detached. I was the girl who had just gotten diagnosed as bipolar. From there, it was all about medication, finding routine, and reducing stress, all to keep away recurring episodes.

What being bipolar has done for me is expose me to different parts of myself that I wouldn't have otherwise explored. It's me, unfiltered. I often find myself asking what parts of me are authentically me, but I'm going about it all wrong. It is all me, every part of it at once. If anything, I have a bigger understanding of myself than others do. I've seen my mind stretch to parts I didn't know existed. I feel emotion with the most intense passion. I shouldn't question my happiness for fear that I'm feeling too much. Sometimes I really didn't know how I felt about something until I experienced moments of uncontrolled enthusiasm.

People often ask me what it's like to live bipolar. In an effort to answer this, I offer the following windows into my bipolar world.

Manic Tree Experience

Growing up, I liked to think of myself as a hippie, running through forests barefoot, flowers in my hair, on the hunt for fairies. I read books in trees and hummed "The Sound of Music." Trailing behind me in my adventures were my neighbourhood friends. We had moved several times, and in each place we moved to I'd claim a "Terabithia," essentially a spot that mimicked the famous forest from the movie *Bridge to Terabithia*. These symbols—forests, flowers, fairies—became themes for me. They are the things I grew up with and knew. During manic episodes, they became accentuated. These are the symbols with which I identified, so it made sense that they appeared so predominantly in manic episodes.

There is a consistent theme of nature in my episodes. It's how I see the world, how I feel connected. In an altered state of mind, I can get lost in a field of flowers and feel at one with them, having no perception of time.

These interests of mine became fascinations in Grade Eight. My love for trees became an obsession. With great clarity, I remember once yearning to jump into a tree. I had just looked out my window and saw tree whispering to me with all its might: "Come, climb." I ran outside and felt a gust of wind on my face. Launching myself off the porch, I followed the wind's cues to the alluring first branch. I grasped the firm branch with my hands and used my monkey legs to walk the trunk. I felt light and airy. Once perched, I giggled into the air. I smiled at the sun. I couldn't explain my exhilaration, but I adored it. I talked aloud into the empty air. I expressed my joyous love for the given moment. I felt my imagination come to life. Each gust of wind disguised itself as a message from God.

I then felt the urge to share this immediate joy with my mother. With all my heightened energy, I located her back in the house. Immense happiness wrote itself across my face as I looked into her eyes. I wrapped my arms around her as my tear ducts filled. I tried to express to her my spiritual experience. She just looked at me and said that she had never seen me happier.

Manic Running

There were times when I couldn't physically keep up with the pace of my thoughts. In an attempt to catch up with them, I took up sporadic running. In the middle of the night, I'd ask to go for runs. I'd run barefoot, in flip flops, you name it. I would run where my feet told me to go. I'd run throughout all the paths of our neighbourhood.

One day while running along one of the forested paths, a memory sparked of my parents telling me that we were going to go to the elementary school fair that evening. I checked my iPod and saw that still had lots of time. So I kept running while trying to come up with solutions to any apparent issues. As fleeting thoughts came and went, I ran right through them. I didn't seem to mind that I'd been running the last hour in flip flops. In that moment, it struck me how mean the kids at school were to our grumpy bus driver. I could see right through her grumpiness. I appreciated her.

I'm going to write her a letter, so she feels loved, I thought.

I stopped mid-run, whipped out my iPod, and wrote a lengthy letter on it. I then gasped at the realization of the time. Without soaking in the reality that there was no chance of getting back home in time for the fair, I picked up and ran, having no shortage of energy.

When I reached the house, it was too late. The family was gone.

No problem there, I thought. *I'll just run to the school.*

I hinged my heels in the opposite direction without sparing a moment. I felt like I was floating. I closed my eyes, taking it all in. I felt like I could do anything. I was like the flying colours on my tie-dyed T-shirt. I stopped to follow dragonflies and butterflies on the way.

When I got to elementary, which was on top of a hill, I discovered that my family had already been there for a bit and were ready to leave. I had just gotten there, though, and I was determined to stay. My family gave up. I stayed, and you can bet I made my own way back.

Manic me at the school fair.

Depression

The first time I remember experiencing depression, it was the summer of Grade Six. I'd had all sorts of plans to go off to camps and visit cousins on my own, things I was initially excited for, but when the time came I felt very anxious. Those nerves resulted in me physically throwing up. I felt as though I were walking through fog, passing through scenes rather than experiencing them. It was almost like something was separating me from everyone else—like a glass wall.

I didn't know how to handle the time away or the overwhelming new events. I remember hiding out in my aunt's attic, watching television when I should have been helping her look after her baby. I would sit on her couch and just be in a daze. I was there physically, but mentally numb.

I was so absentminded that I fell right into the background. She would come up with her baby and I'd be uninterested in interacting with them.

A Mixed Episode

In the spring of Grade Eleven, I encountered one of my hardest episodes yet—a mixed state. I was depressed in the mornings and manic in the evenings. It was incredibly hard to get up in the mornings and motivate myself to go to school. There were times when my parents had to leave for work and couldn't help me get out of bed.

On those days, I'd call on Jack, a friend who lived a block away from us. He was very familiar with my different states, as he'd seen them all.

One morning, I felt like I couldn't lift myself up from my bed. If I stayed in bed, nothing could go wrong, I thought. I rested my hand across my damp face, feeling what felt like permanent tear trails. What was the point in going to school when I knew I couldn't last the day? I rolled over and hugged the sheets as if they could protect me from all harm.

I slipped my hand underneath my covers and grabbed my phone off the bedside table—and called Jack. I gave him the same spiel I'd been using the past week. Without hesitation, he was on his way.

I rolled out of bed and made my way down the stairs. By the time I'd come into the kitchen, he was there. He helped me put together a lunch as I angrily spouted out words of low self-worth. I started to yell; he just let me go at it.

He then asked if I wanted to talk to my friend Emma. I nodded as he dialled and filled Emma in. He proceeded to put her on speaker. She spoke to me calmly and reassuringly while Jack put my bag together. We headed for the door and he walked me to school.

Hallucinations

During my first hospital experience, I had visions and hallucinations. On the night when I was admitted to the ER, I remember sitting on my hospital bed with my legs swinging back and forth. I glanced over to the nurses in the hall, and they had dancing feet and smiles to match. They were angels on earth sent just for me.

Selena Gomez was also being sent just for me. I just knew that she knew. I could sense it! She was aware that one of her fans wasn't well.

I couldn't believe she was coming to see me. I hopped off the hospital bed and walked to the restroom. Inside, I looked into the mirror, took a closer look at myself while drawing water from the tap, and splashed it onto my face.

I could feel her coming.

Selena Gomez

What better cure is there to depression than Selena Gomez? As you've probably read, Selena Gomez is my favourite celebrity, and after my first hospitalization my seventy-five-year-old grandma paid for me to go to her concert. Did I mention that she also accompanied me? My sister and mom came, too, and my grandma treated us all to dinner that night. My sister and I even made posters—and attempted T-shirts!

The concert took place at the Air Canada Centre in Toronto, and we were just a couple rows from the floor. Selena made me feel something that night, something that lifted me out of the numbness of just have been diagnosed as bipolar. It was no wonder I later invited her to the hospital for tea.

Bipolar Rejection

The first Christmas Eve after I was diagnosed, I experienced one of my strongest hallucinations. The night before Christmas, I had started seeing dark figures heckling me from the dark shadows of my room. I started to sing to them to make the voices stop; I would hum my favourites, mostly from *The Sound of Music*.

I couldn't stop shaking and my temperature kept changing. My parents came to rock their fifteen-year-old daughter to sleep and drown out the false noise.

The next morning, I was in another world, having not fully processed the events of the night before. I felt that I must let everyone know just how much I appreciated them. My parents found it necessary to take me to the hospital that morning, even though it was Christmas.

When we got to triage, though, we didn't have the best of luck. At the time, I was on a maintenance drug and had a prescription for another drug that served as an antipsychotic to use as needed. Since I'd only recently been diagnosed, we were still unsure of how many milligrams to take. The staff at the ER just assumed I wasn't taking my meds, and so they rejected me.

This wasn't the last time I'd be rejected from the hospital.

In the spring of 2016, before the first of two hospital visits, I was struggling strongly with suicide ideation. I had gone on a youth retreat and couldn't stop obsessing about suicide. My friend Emma had to continuously soothe me out of this state of mind.

After a few calls with concerned youth leaders, it became clear that I should go to the hospital. At the ER, the staff said that ideation wasn't enough to admit me; I needed to have devised a plan of suicide.

We were distraught that I wasn't sick enough to meet their standard. After much back and forth, and many interviews, I decided, as my last shot, that when they asked what kind of dark thoughts I was having I would say that sometimes I was tempted to reach for the knives in the kitchen drawer. This was finally enough.

Grade Eleven

During my Grade Eleven year, I had many hopes and ambitions. I was determined to be in a school program that took place outside school grounds. It included experiential ways of learning while gaining credits. It was called MADE (Music, Art, Drama, English), and it mainly focused on the arts, something I wasn't very experienced with but wanted to learn.

The lack of structure seemed to throw me off at first. Or maybe I was just trying to accomplish too much. Either way, the stress threw me for a loop and I started to feel my manic, which was my body's natural way of dealing with it.

I remember arriving at MADE one day with so much anxious energy that I couldn't handle it.

In the below journal entry, notice that I am fighting the oncoming mania:

February 13, 2016

So… a new semester has begun. It didn't start the way I had imagined. But nonetheless, there's room for improvement. I am currently in Ottawa at my uncle's, reflecting on what has happened so far. Every day since MADE (an off-campus program that includes music, art, drama, and English) started, I have been having breakdowns. I guess especially because this is a transition with stress and high-pressure situations, plus the season is changing, it was bound to happen. A mental breakdown. I am currently working on fighting off mania and depression and it is hard, but I am determined to stay in MADE. This may not be how I wanted to make an impression, but they will know the real me. And I will experience to the fullest everything this program has to offer. With friends, teachers, and counsellors like mine, I will get through this. Happy is the heart that feels pain they say. I will be back happier with a well-deserved update. There has to be some minor setbacks in life. The keyword is minor.

Unfortunately, when you look at my next entry, made two days later, you will notice that the disorder won.

February 15, 2016

I am sitting on the top floor of my hotel, floor 28, at 5 am. It has a huge line of windows across the back wall. You can see the whole city! Right now, it is a bit dark. So, all the city lights are on and it's just breath-taking. I am going to wait to see the sunrise… the sun has risen, and it is beautiful. You can see big fogs of smoke expanding out of buildings. You can see trees peeking out of neighbourhoods and there are towering buildings everywhere. It is so grand. I walk by each window feeling like I am walking on air. I look down at the mini city. I felt like I was hopping from building to building. I could see above all of the buildings with the smoke building up and up. I was walking on clouds. Each light saying hello to you, illuminating the city.

These "minor" setbacks led me to a couple of hospitalizations that semester. I was discharged from the first hospital visit because I had essentially downplayed my symptoms in order to manipulate the system so I could be released early. But I was still very manic and needed to be there.

I had thought I could go right back to MADE, but that wasn't the case. When I returned to school, I was told that I would have to be enrolled in regular classes. I felt defeated.

I was in a mixed state and my emotions, plans, and ideas changed quickly. I was starting to not be able to handle school. Because I couldn't stay focused in class, I kept skipping them. I would instead go to Jack, who would keep an eye on me.

Since I couldn't sit in class, I spent my days in the guidance counsellors' office. They were aware of my situation and looked out for me. Jack would bring his books down with him and work beside me to keep me sane.

At lunches, I had so much emotion that I could barely sit with my friends. I'd cry so much because I couldn't stop the madness in my head. To get away from the crowded halls, Jack and my friend Hunter would find quiet, less overwhelming places in the school for us to sit. We would go to empty classrooms—even the girl's washroom, where we'd lock the door.

I wanted the pain to go away. Naturally, suicide ideation came into play. I started to vocalize my dark thoughts to Jack, who stopped me mid-track and reminded me that he had my mom's number and wasn't afraid to call.

This didn't stop my scheming thoughts, though. I found myself creating plans to stop eating and drinking in the hope of passing out. I figured this would temporarily solve the pain without any long-term effects.

I forget exactly how long this plan lasted, but the next morning at lunch, my friends were concerned. When they tried to encourage me to eat, I became distressed. My tummy was in knots and I was pale. This was apparent to a couple of friends coming down the hall who swooped down and hauled me to the girl's washroom. A teacher followed behind. Together, they convinced me to eat and drink water, and they gave me fruit. One of the concerned friends stayed with me during her spare.

At that point, I thought I had talked myself out of a suicide attempt, although suicidal thoughts can be recurring in that state.

When the last period bell rang, I met Jack at his locker. We went to his house and played video games. I was very hyper, playing as if I were very drunk. When the time came for me to go home, I wasn't ready and Jack let me stay. He did his homework while I watched music videos. His family offered me dinner when they came home, but I barely touched it. I felt foggy and light-headed. When I went to the washroom, I just stared into the mirror, barely recognizing myself.

I then texted Jack to meet me upstairs and told him that I thought it was urgent that I tell his parents what was going on with me, because I felt unsafe. All of my other friends' parents knew that I was bipolar, and they should know, too. He agreed with me after a little convincing.

At that point, Jack had to go to singing lessons, so I asked if it would be okay if I went along when his mom dropped him off. After she dropped him off, I started to fill her in on everything while she ran errands. She listened thoughtfully at my abrupt revelations and bought me a frozen yogurt. Feeling more at ease, we picked up Jack after his lessons and went back to his house. I stayed a little while longer, until just after nine o'clock when Jack's mom suggested that he walk me home.

As soon as we stepped on the porch, though, the wind swept away all my remaining sanity.

I turned to Jack. "Let's just run away," I said, very seriously. "Let's just go. I want to forget everything. I want to get drunk. I don't care if I'm manic!"

He tried to subtly redirect me.

When we reached my house, I announced I wasn't going in.

"Yes, you are," he said, trying to pull me toward the house. It was approaching ten o'clock at night.

Now for my power move: I turned to the street, walked right into the middle of it, sat down, and crossed my arms.

"I'm not getting up," I stated strongly.

"You're going to get hit by a car," he said.

"Well, maybe I want to."

"Josée, there are a lot of things I would do for you, but I can't be a part of this." He pulled out his phone. "I won't hesitate to call your mom if I have to."

"Fine."

Then I stood up and starting to seat, lashing out at him.

It was a struggle getting back to the house, and he had to play tricks on me, making deals to get me to go inside. When I was finally in the house, Jack quickly noted to my parents that they should keep an eye out.

It wasn't long before I went right back to the hospital.

Exceptional Nurses

Over the years, there have been some noteworthy things that nurses have gone out of their way to help us with.

One incident that stands out to me is when I needed to go to the hospital for the second time in the spring of 2016. I agreed to go back, as long as it was on my terms. I came up with a list of conditions that had to be met before I could come back. I don't remember the list in its entirety, but it included being able to wear makeup, shave, and listen to music.

At midnight, I found myself sitting with a nurse and my dad in the hospital room, sorting out what was reasonable. The nurse agreed to my list and made some concessions in my favour. This made the transition a lot easier, as it made me feel like I had some say.

I spent an awful lot of time while I was in the hospital creating new hairdos.

Hey Josée,

Hope that you are getting the help that you need to be who you really are. And I am praying for you every day and I hope that you can come home soon as my beautiful and loving sister.

From Luke

A heart-warming letter Luke sent me while I was in the hospital.

Manic Rollerblading

During a manic episode in the spring of 2016, I determined to go rollerblading down by the river. Before reaching the river, you have to go down an incredibly steep hill—and at the time there was rush hour traffic. Of course, there were other ways to get to the river, but in my manic state I dismissed them.

So I strapped on my rollerblades and headed down the hill at full speed. I felt exuberantly confident until I had to make an abrupt stop. Only I didn't know how. I latched onto the only object in sight, the yellow safety guard of a nearby hydro pole. When I grabbed onto the safety guard, I whipped under it like the undertow of a wave.

A concerned biker passing by and asked if I was okay. I assured him that everything was fine and proceeded to dust myself off.

Just a few minor scratches, I thought as blood streamed down my leg. *I'll just stop at the boathouse and ask for a first aid kit.*

I continued down the hill towards the river, rollerblading as though there was nothing wrong.

When I reached the boathouse, I went in with my rollerblades and asked for a first aid kit. They gave me a box and told me to help myself to a bandage.

I proceeded to rollerblade for another hour before I got lost, at which time I called for my parents to pick me up. And let me tell you, it is no easy feat to explain where you are when you really have no idea.

Manic rollerblading.

Spring 2016

In the process of getting me situated at CAIP, the hospital didn't have any beds for me, so I had to stay in the holding unit—not a fun place. The place was practically overflowing with less-experienced nurses. There were patients there with dementia who were taking off their clothes because they were confused, patients who were experiencing constant hallucinations, patient with short tempers, and everything in between.

The holding unit consisted of about four rooms. That may seem small, but trust me when I say it was a happening place. The rooms were lined with windows, so that the patients could be observed. There was very little privacy. In the room where I was placed, there was simply a bed with a table attached to the wall and a chair connected to the floor. Nothing else except for messages scrawled across the walls from the fiery hands of past patients. Worst thing of all, I couldn't see outside, let alone be outside.

Outside of these four rooms, the orderlies worked away in the centre of it all, which was essentially a glass case. From there, they observed, recorded, and enforced rule upon rule. There was one washroom. I took long showers because it was the only place where I had privacy—at least, that was my perception. I would sit and just let the water drown out my tears.

The nurses went through everything I'd brought and determined whether it was safe, whether I could harm myself or others with it. They confiscated my hardcover books and cut my bookmark strings. Even underwire bras were an issue. No elastics or drawstrings were allowed. Trust me, they didn't take many risks.

Keep in mind, though, that this was just a holding space, so the rules had to be broader than in other parts of the hospital. In my room, I had nowhere to put the things I had left. I just set my clothes in a corner.

When my parents came to visit, they asked who I wanted to see. Jack was the name that escaped from my lips. They granted that wish and showed up with him next time. Piled high in Jack's hands were copies of *National Geographic*, my favourite. Of course, the nurse had to stop him and check his bag.

I don't often hug Jack, because he's not very fond of hugs, but I really needed a hug. When he put the magazines aside and gave me his full attention, I asked him about Shane Koyczan, a spoken word poet whose show I had been looking forward to attend. I'd planned to go with Jack and my friends Amy and Hunter. I had paid and everything, but the hospital had intruded on my plans.

Jack said that they hadn't been able to find anybody to take my ticket, so they'd given up and passed it along to a security officer. Not much later, someone by the name of Josh had been looking for a ticket and the security guard gave him mine. Josh happened to be a good friend of Amy's. He also happened to be my future first boyfriend.

The whole time Jack was relaying this to me, I couldn't stop thinking about how perfectly this had all played out. We talked about other things I simply can't remember. I do recall him noticing my underwear in the corner, because there was nowhere to put it. We identified the messages on the walls and talked about other patients and all the rules. He even read aloud from my favourite teen romance novel—in funny accents and exaggerated expressions, of course. It was priceless. He made me feel like I had a bit of home with me.

Mall Visit

When I was in Kitchener, during my mixed state, Jack came by for another visit. I had an off-unit pass, and we used it to go to the mall. I was very excited to be off-unit. We started by getting some food, which I was very happy about because I wouldn't have to eat another hospital meal.

Afterward, Dad let Jack and me pave our own path. I dragged him into store after store to look for a birthday gift for my friend Amber. I was hyper and relentless. He bought me ice cream and bought Amber's gift for me, too.

I had a gift card to Aerie, a bra and underwear store and I was very determined to go in. Of course, Jack wasn't too keen about it. I dragged him in anyway. After I bought what I wanted, though, I realized that I needed tampons—another place Jack wasn't so keen on visiting. You can bet I brought him in anyway.

Out of My Skin

It is so quiet… I can't bear it, but it almost brings
a sense of comfort. It smells thickly of hand
sanitizer and sympathy. You can feel the hands of
sadness wrapped around you filling extra space
like molecules. You can clearly see the outlines
of safety. Funny how they make it so safe, even
though you are in a hospital. You can almost
feel the hurt and confusion in someone's eyes. I
knew eyes were powerful, but not that powerful.
And hearing is a funny thing. You can hear
the soft blows of a fan, doors closing but never
locking, and socks making a peeling sound as
the stickers come off the ever so glossy floor. You
feel as though you have to watch everything you
do. Like you can't even trust yourself. I mean,
you are being observed, right? I know this is
supposed to help, but not having anyone familiar
around you carries great difficulty. It forces
connection with people and nurses, which isn't
such a bad thing. It is just hard going around
without knowing your surroundings. I just want
to be home. In a way, I feel more anxious here.
But not in the way I normally feel nerves. I just
want to be outside and cope with nerves the
way I know how. I feel trapped here. Untrusted.
Unusually untrusted. I mean, it makes me feel
grateful I guess to discover new coping strategies.
It is proving to be difficult though. I know
they are just helping, and looking for the right
medication for me, but I cannot help but feel like
an experiment.

—Josée Leclair

29. JACK'S STORY

Jack

Before we talk about Josée, I think it's important to understand the context, the alternative education program in which we met, CELP.

The C stands for community. In theory, this means frequent team-building activities, lots of group work, and lessons on interdisciplinary studies. But in execution, the sense of community comes from the flexible day structure that allows for ample time for students to just "chill." It comes from lazing about on a hot day or gossiping in a cabin. It comes from wandering down to the creek or exploring the woods, making food for lunch or wrestling in the leaves. This is the simple genius of how CELP knits a random group of classmates so incredibly close. Given space, time, and no distractions, kids will independently come together as a community.

The E stands for environment, which refers to the forest setting and scheduled bike and canoe trips. Birthed from this, though, are the long and in-depth discussions that happen so often on subject like sustainable farming, global warming and climate change, the dairy industry, invasive species, mass extinctions, coral reefs, and water bottles—to name a few.

The L is for leadership. The program is sold to the school board to emphasize that the students will engage in lessons, volunteer in the community, and teach fifth-graders about the environment, but once again leadership comes more from the program's overall freedom. Students have the freedom to play like little children again, and in a backwards and bizarre way this liberty to optimize how you play or do homework makes you feel more like an adult than anything else. And from this drastic and immediate responsibility over one's own time springs leadership qualities.

Finally, the P stands for program. That's kind of self-explanatory.

Personally, I filled out the CELP application the day before it was due largely on a whim. Now it's hard to think about how life would have been different if I'd missed CELP. The program affected the lives of almost every kid who passed through it, and it certainly affected mine in many ways, not least of which is that I met Josée.

I clearly remember meeting Josée in the same way you remember an embarrassing blunder, your first bike ride, or a prestigious recognition. It felt innately significant.

To be clear, this wasn't really the first time I'd "met" Josée, in the sense that I had physically laid eyes on the freckled, curly-haired girl before. But it is the moment when she became a distinct person in my life, more than a name.

CELP is so different from traditional educational methods that the school board even allows sleepovers. A few times per semester, the class squishes into a cabin, spreading an interlocking jigsaw of sleeping bags across the floor. The nights are spent gossiping, cooking, and hushing up quickly if the teacher is nearby.

At the time, I was attempting to complete something called National Novel Writing Month—or NaNoWriMo, for short, if you can call that short. The challenge is to write a fifty-thousand-word novel in one month. Every day you log how many words you write, with the recommended quota being two thousand. If you fall behind, the next day you have to write four thousand, or six thousand, and pretty soon you're trapped behind a never-ending wall of unrealized, unachievable word counts.

Which is why, at around 9:00 p.m. one evening, I tore myself away from the excitement to retreat to the back corner of the cabin to write two thousand words. Our teacher Sarah (we referred to her by her first name only, another testament to the unique teaching style of CELP) directed me to use the first bedroom on the right as a quiet spot. Being dyslexic, I promptly entered the first bedroom on the left.

Flicking on the light, I noticed the drab wallpaper, dusty desk, and a blanketed figure on the bed. It was Josée. I don't remember her squinting or rubbing her eyes, so I'm not totally sure she had been asleep when I came in. She just rolled over and looked at me.

The room was pretty small, and most of it was taken up by a big board of CELP photos, so I just sat down at the foot of the bed.

Being the gentlemen that I was, I said, "I gotta do some writing" and planted myself on the bed. I suppose I wasn't super tactful back in Grade Ten, because I launched into how I was writing this book and needed "just a second to write." She very politely asked what the book was about. Until that point, I hadn't verbalized what the book *was* about—not out of sheepishness or from lack of artistic clarity; it was just that no one had bothered to ask.

"It's kind of a collection of short stories," I explained. "But they're all sort of linked together. Well, most of them are… and they tell the story of humanity."

It was to be a sprawling historical space epic, told through brief vignettes of different characters' experiences. Together the stories would recount pivotal moments in mankind's history, mixing truth and fiction, past and far future. I thought it would be a good idea because I could avoid stalling by jumping between different short stories. But in practice, I just ran out of ideas faster.

Since I figured I would be looking at a blank page for a long time, I asked Josée what she thought were some pivotal moments in history, preferably ones that exhibited humanity at its deepest and most basic level. Looking back, it was kind of a heavy topic to lead with.

The discussion ended up being more about me talking and Josée acting as a blank canvas to bounce ideas off of. She mostly just shrugged, smiled awkwardly, or nodded along as I talked, but eventually we made the following list:

- A man tried for something is put in the iron bull in ancient Rome.
- A mother singing "My Bonny Lies Over the Ocean" to her dying daughter.

- A spaceship being blown up by some future weapon (like an atom bomb).
- What a mom gets her daughter for all her birthdays before the mother's untimely death.
- A man gets a wish to live forever from a genie. He later regrets this as life becomes tedious if you don't die.
- A person stands in front of a tank.
- Aliens are deciding the fate of humanity and are reviewing their best and worst moments. They also have a spokesperson who is human and can live forever.
- A group of people who mysteriously disappeared in the present are trying to rob a future bank.
- A little girl selling rainbows.
- The story of the guy who stopped lead poisoning.
- Humans destroy an entire planet just to get to its core.
- Stalin stuff.

I don't remember who exactly said what, although a few of these ideas are definitely mine. I can't imagine Josée coming up with "Stalin stuff," for example. In the same way, I can't see myself coming up with "A little girl selling rainbows."

Eventually though, she said, "Okay Jack, I have to go to sleep."

"Why are you going to sleep while everyone is awake?"

"I have a mental condition so I need sleep."

"Doesn't really answer my question."

"Well, I have bipolar."

Josée would tell me years later that she only said this to get me to leave. I guess it really backfired, because I was very intrigued about what "bipolar" was and started asking her about it. She explained about mania and the corresponding depression and the haziness surrounding both. For me, hearing about it for the first time, my thoughts went from "Oh, so it's kind of like Gollum" to "Oh, this is, ummmm… significant."

At that point, I had an idea which seemed genius to me. I naturally thought a story about a bipolar girl could fit compatibly into my sprawling epic, and I asked her if I could use this in a short story.

"Umm, sure, as long as you don't mention my name."

Pretty soon I had a pencil in my hand and a notepad in my lap. I started asking her—or more accurately, interviewing her—about anything and everything to do with being bipolar. She explained how hard it was for her family, how she felt like she couldn't do anything, how embarrassed she was after being manic, and how it all just seemed completely random.

Once I had a page of notes, I said, "I should probably let you get some sleep."

And I left.

I never did let her read the chapter with the bipolar character, despite her constant insistence. It ended up a strange mixture of overconfidence, incoherence, and rampant insensitivity. Essentially, the problem I had writing it back in Grade Ten is the same problem I wrestle with today: the impossibility of imagining the fluid and life-altering mental state that Josée described to me that day.

Over the years, Josée and I have become really good friends, and in that time I have observed Josée experience a huge range of emotions—joy to despair, shame to anticipation, and every shade in between. Emotions too complex or exact to be described. It's like some huge "feelings" paintbrush is constantly mixing new shades, stopping only briefly before moving on to the next creation, all the time carrying the previous residue with it. Often Josée will use analogies to try and pinpoint for me what she's experiencing. She'll try to shift through the haze and capture a particular feeling in words before it's gone. But attempting to fully impart those feelings to me, even if she had the perfect analogy, is futile.

I like to think of this way. Birds can see in the ultraviolent spectrum of light, meaning they perceive more colours than humans do, colours completely inconceivable to humans. Being non-bipolar and trying to imagine what it's like to be bipolar is akin to imagining a new colour through the lens of a bird. Which is why my story, written in the point of view of someone with bipolar, was… bad.

But that story, and by extension that conversation in the cabin, taught me something important. When I'm in a situation where Josée cries for no discernible reason, or starts to laugh uncontrollably, I just remind myself that she "sees" differently. And I would be lying if I said I wasn't curious about what that would be like. I'm not sure if it's the right way to think about it, but it works for me.

Morning Awakening

The sunlight pours out of my window
Lighting up my bedroom
I can feel the light change around me
My eyes start to flutter open
I pull my covers in and give them a squeeze
I release the covers and swing myself into an
upright position
I sit looking out the window letting my thoughts
of reality come back to me
I start to feel the heat of the sun on my cheeks
The sky is screaming blue and is lightly touched
with a few feathered clouds
I breathe in the present moment
I feel ready to start the day

—Josée Leclair

30. OTHER PEOPLE WHO HAVE IMPACTED MY LIFE

Josée

THE RYANS. IN CELP, I MET THE RYAN TRIPLETS—CLARA WITH HER quiet confidence, Amy with her feisty determination, and Maggie with her spunky personality. I first connected with Amy, as she was in my leadership group for earth-keepers, teaching environmental sciences to kids. Clara was on the quieter side and Maggie was in the adjoining class.

One day on a bus ride home, I wasn't having a good time holding myself together; it was one of my off days. Seeing that I was in tears, Amy offered to take me out for hot chocolate, and this is when I let her in on my struggle with bipolar disorder. She was very understanding and lent me a listening ear.

During this time, my family was making a move from the south end to downtown and I was trying to decide if I wanted to switch schools. A lot of the friends I'd made in CELP went to the school I was considering. Jack, along with the Ryans, did some convincing and won me over.

I really started to relate to Clara going into the school year; she was similar to me in character. Every day she and I sat together at lunch, and sometimes one of her sisters would join us. We did that for the next couple of years. I didn't really make friends outside of the Ryans.

When I was enrolled in MADE in Grade Eleven, all three of them were in the program as well. As this was the peak of my mixed episode, I leaned on them a lot. I had frequent panic attacks and they always ended up being the ones to ground me again.

But without meaning to, I was making my problems other people's. They felt as though they had to constantly check if I was okay. At a later time, Amy approached me about needing to be more independent. I couldn't be dependent on them anymore or expect them to make decisions for me. She told me that she didn't want to worry about if I was okay all the time. She reminded me they weren't going to be in school next year.

"Don't take this the wrong way," she said. "We love you and will continue being your friend, but you need to expand your wings."

I hadn't meant to hold them back. They had done what was best, and they had done it out of love. I'll always appreciate their strong-willed and diverse characters.

Nicola. I originally met Nicola in Girl Guides, although we were then disconnected for a couple of years—until we found ourselves together again in high school. We picked up where we had left off.

Nicola had a relatable sense of character. I always felt at home with her, and she was always able to understand where I was at. She was there for me at times when I really needed her, from phones calls to hospital visits. In one interesting turn of events, I stayed at her house for a few days while my family moved us downtown. I wasn't doing so well, as I hadn't slept the first night. She had given me the bed while she slept on the floor, but she'd ended up cuddling me to sleep as I sobbed.

That night threw me off and I became a little high. I remember making Christmas cards in a manic frenzy in her basement, but Nicola took it like a pro, getting up to my level and giving me all the supplies I needed to make the best holiday cards.

Over the years, she's called some pretty important shots, like when I called her at 7:00 a.m. the morning after threatening suicide with Jack. She had to make the heavy decision to let my mom know that I should go to the hospital.

She visited me when I was in CAIP. We sat in the hospital cafeteria as she provided a familiar face. We talked and laughed like nothing was wrong. I told her that we weren't supposed to swear in the unit, but also that I really needed to let it out.

"Then do it," she said, giving me the space I needed to be vulnerable.

Nicola always accepted me and gave me what I needed to be myself.

A Mid-Morning Swing

I find myself at the swings on this lovely
morning
I dig the back of my heels into the sand and
swing myself back and forth
I feel the wind lift the ends of my hair as I let
myself go higher and higher
Pumping my legs with more force, I start to
catch speed
I feel like I could reach out and touch a cloud
I squeeze my eyes shut and imagine myself flying
I get ready for blast off as I go up, I push off and
make a landing

—Josée Leclair

31. THE ART OF MANIA

Josée

THOSE WHO KNOW ME KNOW THAT I TAKE MUCH PLEASURE IN writing and taking pictures. If one were to ask when I realized these passions, the honest answer is that it was sparked by my first manic episode. When I was first experiencing mania, I took creative photos and wrote a lot of poems. That was when I really discovered I enjoyed these interests.

Sometimes it can be hard to decipher whether the desires you have while mania are true to you. I believe that these were always my passions, just waiting to escape and be enhanced. They continue to drive me outside of the mania. Being born of mania doesn't make them any less valid to who I am as a person. When I picked up running, it was part of a manic dream. But with my art, it reveals the real me. I believe that it is defining.

My interest in painting has a lot of relevance to my first boyfriend, Josh. When we first met, he asked me to dance on a rooftop. I had so many feelings in the midst of this, feeling I was experiencing for the first time. Those feelings were so strong that they have stuck with me.

That Christmas, I was starting to dip into mania again—like most Christmases. As it all crept back, I felt as though I had to make an art piece that encompassed my relationship with Josh. So I grabbed the acrylics from my sister's room and didn't even bother to change out of my white sweater. I painted wisps off a canvas while including swerves of poetry that I felt captured exactly how I felt.

Dating someone with bipolar disorder is hard. They may ask you out on a manic whim, for example. They may run off impulsively to look at something more enticing than you. They may obsessively and passionately describe points of interest to you. They may perseverate on something you already let go. They may cry for a reason that isn't obvious to you. They may express too much emotion or too little. They may suddenly become giddier than usual. They may struggle to depict the madness inside.

All of this to say: be prepared to be taken through the impulsive whims of their minds!

If you're bipolar and going into your first relationship, know that you will have many initial fears—the fear of not being accepted, of the other person not understanding the erratic states of your mood, of them liking you more when you're manic, or of thinking you *are* the mania or the depression.

With Josh, I feared these things unnecessarily. Time after time, Josh demonstrated that these moods didn't faze him. From literally the first time we hung out, I felt comfortable in confiding to him that I was bipolar. Typically I don't tell someone that so quickly, but something was different about him; he made me feel safe enough to tell him. I somehow just knew this person was someone I could trust.

As with most people's reactions when I tell them, he was naturally curious as to the nature of the disorder. And as predicted, he came to know some of my different states of being. Christmas in particular exemplified the widest range of my emotions. I was in and out of hypomanic states and experiencing minor depression. Josh handled both really well.

One year, we invited Josh to join us in our tradition of going to the cottage to visit my extended family. At this point, I was experiencing a bit of a low. I was emotionally sensitive and hitting peaks of exhaustion during the drive. When Josh started receiving texts from a mutual friend about her new pregnancy, I was caught a little off-guard. This was someone whose emotions I sometimes took on.

Throughout the car ride, Josh was my comfort and my pillow. At different times of the weekend I became overwhelmed and had to retreat to another room. Josh respected my space and texted to check in while he played with my cousins. At one point during a dinner, I felt that I couldn't handle it and went upstairs. Mom was about to go after me, but Josh told her he'd look after it. He just sat beside me and soothed my thoughts while I snuggled in a blanket on the bed.

He took me on lots of walks through the snow to lighten my mood. When deep exhaustion hit me, I threw myself onto the couch. Josh introduced me to cuddling, which also lightened my low.

After Christmas, the mood shifts continued, bouncing between exhaustion and little highs. On New Year's Eve, I wanted to do it all, including Chinese food, fireworks, and a midnight party. I was feeling manic into the night and knew I should take meds, but I took the wrong one.

Josh handled the night very well as he simply went along with my plans. He had kissed me for the first time the day before, and this night I was so exhausted that I just fell into his chest, almost asleep, wrapped in a blanket with the lights out.

In later months, I exhibited periods of impulsivity and continued to ask him questions such as what he noticed about my behaviour, seeking clues to my mania. He supported me and accompanied me to my mental health talks and went along with all my whims. He was a consistent listening ear. Josh gave me amazing memories and I will always be so grateful that he was my first boyfriend.

Reflection

My tear-filled eyes explored my reflection in my Christmas-lit mirror, not necessarily because it was Christmas, but because the lights comforted me. Dotted along my glossy irises grew reflectors of the surrounding light, tears rooted from nowhere specific, perhaps a place of longing of where I'm from. My cheeks appeared flushed, my freckles were light in shade—not like when I come from the sun—and my lashes clung together from the rain. I felt relieved to see my tears. They gave me assurance of my pure feeling, making me think that I just needed this moment, to be simply present, to not try and dissect my lingering tears. They were sent for me.

It's not unusual to see me tear up. I feel things twice as intensely as others. I have no line of separation. Others can store their feelings, but I'm like a leaking faucet. I cry when I'm happy, when I'm sad, and when I'm angry. Tears are my emotional outlet. I cry when I'm moved, and I'm touched by little things. Sometimes I'm annoyed by this, but it means that I'm on a deeper level of feeling. I absorb it all.

I'm not afraid to feel, as most are. It's almost a sixth sense. I was never afraid of sadness. I believe that sadness brings out the purest emotion. It's when you're most raw that you come to realizations and epiphanies. All the best songs were born from sadness; you need it to be happy, and that's why it should be embraced. Sadness means something to you.

Confidence

In my bipolar history, I have displayed many situations of exuberant confidence. Like while in the midst of my first manic state, when I declared that I needed more bikinis. I modelled in front of the mirror in my underwear, thinking I had never looked better. I claimed to myself that I needed more underwear, so I proceeded to purchase more than necessary.

Or there was the time when I insisted on taking the perfect photo of a building, so I backed into a line of traffic. Another time I went to a friend's play in my butterfly pyjamas, because I thought I looked awesome; I stayed up until 2:00 a.m. that night playing 21 Questions with Jack, asking things I'd never thought I would say until my manic mouth was born. This wasn't the first time I had confidently let my manic mouth run. Once, when O Canada was playing before school, I couldn't stop loudly relaying commentary back and forth to Jack. Apparently, the teacher kept giving us dagger eyes, but I of course didn't notice this. She marched over, and I burst into tears. We ended up in the guidance office for the next two periods.

Most memorably to me, while babysitting my neighbour's little boys I came to believe that there were messages in the sand revealing our futures. So I dragged them to different parks to analyze the messages. I was a fun babysitter, because I was very childlike myself. I would bring them into my manic world.

Speaking of neighbours, I once expressed interest in a teenage boy who lived nearby, and I pursued him confidently in my manic state. He became such a fascination. My manic whims of confidence never failed to bring me into unexpected situations.

Bipolar Recipes

Over the years since my diagnosis, I have gone through a lot of meds—ones that make my weight change, slow my pace of thought, and give me bigtime food cravings.

The antipsychotics heighten my cravings. Dairy, including sour cream and cheese, are my constant go to. For the foods I already love, I have no self-control—like the time at Christmas when I ate my fair share of poutine and continued to snack on the rest of the family's. I've come up with some wild concoctions—and at weird hours of the night. Usually midnight.

Here are a few of my most memorable recipes:

Club Soda Cocktail
+ I emptied club soda emptied into a tall glass.
+ I added a squirt of honey.
+ And maple syrup.
+ And sugar, both brown and white.
+ And fruit juice.
+ And yes, I drank the whole thing!

Dessert in Two Minutes
+ I placed Oreo crumbs in a bowl.
+ I added peanut butter.
+ And honey.
+ And sugar.
+ And butter.
+ I mixed it all together and enjoyed!

Applesauce and More
+ Start with applesauce.
+ Then add peanut butter.
+ And honey.
+ And sweetener.
+ Mix well and don't get too sticky!

An Afternoon Journal

I sit underneath this grand tree
As I listen to the sound of its leaves in the wind
I pull out my brown leather journal and begin to
write
I feel my hand drift along the page creating a
formation of words
The words start to create a meaning beyond first
looks
They teach me things I did not know about
myself
They show me I have more to offer
With a pen in hand I can open wonders

—Josée Leclair

32. A CLINICAL PERSPECTIVE

Dr. Edwards

I HAVE HAD THE PLEASURE OF GETTING TO KNOW THE LECLAIRS AS A family since 2013. Throughout more than one hundred clinical encounters, I have borne witness to their journey as they navigated through the diagnosis and course of Josée's illness experience, followed by the full pronouncement of Luke's illness experience in 2017.

Josée. My first encounter with the Leclair family was on August 16, 2013 in my child and adolescent psychiatry office. Josée was fifteen years old and had recently been discharged from her first admission to the inpatient child psychiatry unit. She had been hospitalized for an eight-day period and was given a diagnosis of bipolar disorder—the most recent episode was manic with psychotic features. She described her pre-hospital state as a "mental breakdown" in which she felt overwhelmed and emotionally distressed, was unable to make decisions, and had suicidal thoughts. Her emotions and thoughts were "all over the place" and had been preceded for several months by problems with her peer relationships. Her mood disturbance affected her concentration, and insomnia was prominent. Her mood was initially low, and she was tearful much of the time. Excessive, irrational worry and anxiety were also chronic challenges for Josée. Her increased anxiety often led to appetite reduction and vomiting.

Her treatment in hospital consisted of pharmacological management (lithium carbonate and olanzapine) as well as groups for self-esteem and anxiety. At the time of our first meeting, she was being treated with olanzapine (10 mg) and lithium carbonate (900 mg) daily. Since initiation of her medication, Josée felt that her thoughts became more organized, collected, and she was sleeping better. She also increased her physical activity by running, rollerblading, and riding her bike.

Important dates for the development of symptoms throughout her life included "depression" since the age of four, anxiety ever since a family trip at the age of twelve, and mania (racing thoughts, decreased need for sleep, excessive energy, elevated and expansive mood) at the age of fifteen (May 2013).

The development of her first manic episode occurred at a key transitional time in her life, as she was preparing to enter high school that fall. School had always been a source of high stress for her and she had previously been identified as having challenges with her cognition, memory, and central auditory processing.

Over the next few months, Josée's mood remained stable, but she developed undesirable side effects to treatment—namely, significant weight gain from olanzapine and its accompanying physical changes. Simultaneously, Josée was attempting to develop into a young woman, navigate entrance to high school, and manage adolescent social dynamics. She required frequent reminders from her parents to take things slow and access her resources for support. We were able to slowly taper the olanzapine so as to reduce the accompanying sedation and appetite effects.

Josée experienced frustration with the limitations this illness gave to her, as she had to modify her plans around overnight group events because of how sensitive her mood stability was to sleep deprivation. She also experienced guilt and shame when made aware of posts that she had made on social media during episodes of mania and hypomania.

Josée managed well with gradual olanzapine discontinuation and was ecstatic with the healthy weight loss that followed. She was connected with a therapist in the community to assist in her development of skills and strategies to reduce the impact of mood and anxiety challenges.

Throughout Josée's adolescence, she and her family learned to understand the triggers and high-risk circumstances for her illness, and the subtle changes in mood and thought content and process that signalled that she was on the cusp of another episode. Specific recurrent events were also identified as high-probability triggers for episodes. One such event is renting a cottage in Eastern Ontario and spending the holidays with her relatives from Quebec. Every year, due to reduced sleep, change in schedule, and increased stimulation, Josée experienced hypomania that approached mania. Despite the clear effects on her mood and stability, she highly enjoyed those visits and insisted on continuing the tradition. Therefore, we made a plan on an annual basis in advance of their trip such that "as needed" medications were available for use and clear directions were provided to her parents.

Several months before turning eighteen, changes had to be made to Josée's medication regimen due to abnormalities that were detected in routine laboratory investigations. Lithium was slowly changed to Lurasidone, which was relatively new to the Canadian market and was approved for use in adolescents with bipolar disorder. Unfortunately, Josée experienced increasing mood destabilization over the subsequent few months and another mood stabilizer, Epival, was added. Her condition continued to destabilize, and this culminated in the necessity for another acute hospitalization for a manic episode. By this point in her development, the ramifications of her mania-induced behaviour played out in interactions with peers, their families, and in school. Somewhat mercifully, mania appears to protect the affected party by impairing their awareness during the episode, and their memories of the events are often described as hazy or completely absent. This same cannot be said for the witnesses, unfortunately. Thus, after discharge, Josée had to face her friends, their families, and her classmates in a state of only partial awareness of what had transpired.

During her last hospitalization, I conducted a thorough chart review. Her condition was not improving, and her functional impairment was significant. She was overwrought with anxiety about school and her future, unable to make decisions, and was suffering from ongoing mood instability. I discovered anomalies in her laboratory investigations throughout the year that suggested the abnormalities seen previously may not have been attributed to lithium. She had a clear history of lithium responsiveness, and it was suggested to her treating team that she be restarted on lithium. She was discharged a few days later with an adjusted school plan, as well as a medication regimen that included Epival and low-dose lithium carbonate. She continued to improve with increases in her lithium dosage until she achieved remission.

Her anxiety persisted, however. She was given a short course of medication to help her manage anxiety such that she could successfully navigate school; however, I was reluctant to start an antidepressant to target anxiety due to her recent manic episode. She reconnected with a counsellor from a local mental health agency, but that was not a therapeutic experience and Josée opted to discontinue their sessions. She has since made a good connection with a different therapist in the community.

After turning eighteen, Josée faced several additional challenges—she was unsuccessful in her application to her college of choice and experienced her first romantic relationship and subsequent breakup. During that year, her fifteen-year-old brother Luke was also hospitalized for his first manic episode with psychotic features. He was hospitalized for three months, and the family experienced a significant amount of turmoil throughout his episode.

While accompanying Josée on this journey, I have seen her evolve from a scared young adolescent who had to figure out how this illness was going to impact her life going forward, to a young woman who knew what she wanted and boldly set clear intentions for her future. She is taking steps to make that happen, but continues to struggle with anxiety and difficulty managing stress. She has a lot of strengths and is cultivating things that she loves, like reading and writing. A clear measure of wellness and stability for Josée has always been her ability to sit and read a book.

Luke. I first met Luke on February 4, 2015 after Melody arranged for a referral from his pediatrician because of the family's concerns about his history of mood instability. He'd had a diagnosis of ADHD since the age of eight, as well as learning disabilities in reading fluency and writing skills. His family was hyperaware of mood changes and wanted him assessed in case there were early signs of bipolar disorder.

From the start, Luke's personality filled the room—he was ebullient, dynamic, and animated. He provided a history that certainly supported a diagnosis of ADHD, but his mood symptoms were more subtle. For Luke, his shifts in mood were represented by episodes of heightened sensitivity and reactivity—separate from dysregulation that can occur with

ADHD. His parents provided clear details of illustrative examples that had occurred in the previous several months. Luke was somewhat resistant to acknowledge the shifts and had justifications for his reactions. Despite his explanations, there was a clear pattern that existed that resulted in changes in his functionality, reactivity, and ability to reason for circumscribed episodes of time.

Although he had never experienced a clearly defined episode of *mania*, based on the episodic pattern of his subtle mood changes and the family history of Josée's illness I felt comfortable making a presumptive diagnosis of bipolar disorder. Although Melody and Serge had their suspicions, hearing the words spoken out loud by a medical professional seemed to knock the wind out of them. Because of the degree of impairment that his episodes of hypersensitivity were causing him, as it applied to his peer relationships, ability to work in groups in school, managing perceived slights, and ability to tolerate delays in his agenda, a trial of lithium carbonate was initiated.

For several months, Luke argued the diagnosis, stating that he had never experienced anything like Josée had. It was explained repeatedly that the illness can present differently in different people, and although he had never experienced a full manic episode, he had experienced clear episodes of hypersensitivity.

Luke became connected with the counsellor Josée had seen for a brief time at the local mental health clinic. The connection was made to help Luke work on elements of his reactivity, including challenges that occurred on a regular basis in his low tolerance of adversity that affected his ability to work with peers. On one occasion, without consultation with me, this counsellor invited Josée to one of Luke's sessions so he could tell her the negative effect that she'd had on him during her manic and mixed-mood episodes. It should be noted that this was done at a time when Josée had not fully recovered from one of her episodes, and it was not a helpful session for her. In fact, it resulted in significant guilt and more tension between her and Luke.

Risperidone was added to Luke's medication regimen to assist with racing thoughts and difficulty falling asleep. It was incrementally adjusted as needed when sleep disturbance, irritability, and night-time racing thoughts were issues of concern.

Late in 2016, the decision was made to wean Luke from lithium carbonate since he had not experienced a manic episode, although his episodic reactivity and hypersensitivity had been somewhat muted by lithium. Within two weeks of the reduction in his dose of lithium (not even enough time for complete discontinuation), Luke presented with symptoms of acute mania and paranoia. Melody sent a frantic email with a description of his symptoms, and I encouraged her to bring him to the hospital. Within the next few days, Luke's condition deteriorated to a state of frantic psychotic mania in which he was convinced he had been struck by lightning (which fortunately led him to agree to go to the hospital for evaluation). This period of frenetic hysteria caused a significant disturbance for everyone else in the family as well. They were facing the certain reality of a second child with bipolar disorder in the family.

Luke was assessed at the Guelph General Hospital and subsequently transferred to the same child psychiatry unit at Grand River General Hospital that his sister had been admitted to several times. On the inpatient unit, he required seclusion on a number of occasions and received injections of antipsychotic and sedative medications. He was not permitted to see his parents during times of elevated dysregulation. Following injections of haloperidol, he experienced a severe dystonic reaction. After a couple of weeks of no improvement despite receiving high dosages of olanzapine, I suggested to Melody that she inform the treating physician that Luke was responsive to risperidone. Within days of restarting risperidone, Luke's behaviour settled to a point at which he no longer required sedation and was able to partake in unit programming. After another few weeks, he was transferred to the Parkwood Institute in London, where he remained for treatment for six weeks. Throughout that time, I continued to meet with Melody on a regular basis for support.

Luke returned to school for the end of Grade Ten. He has stabilized well on his medications and we have been able to restart Concerta for ADHD since his lithium dosage is adequate. The tremor he developed following the dystonic reaction is resolved and he spends a lot of time with his friends. He still has periods in which he disputes his diagnosis and is excessively critical of his mother. Degree of irritability appears to be a clinical indicator of his illness.

Luke and Josée (and Karina). Two children, one family, one diagnosis. Two children who had severe mental illnesses that caused significant disruption and distress in the family. Suddenly Serge and Melody were in full-time management mode—needing to monitor how everyone was doing at all times, making sure one was not triggering the other, or that illness episodes weren't sneaking up on them. They also had to make sure that their middle child, Karina, was not getting lost or left behind in the wake of her siblings' bipolar illnesses. Extensive plans were made to prepare for Luke's discharge after his three-month hospitalization. This included the household, his siblings, and the school. Stress was palpable on a daily basis and everyone appeared to deal with it in their own way. Karina created a school project about her experience with two ill siblings. Melody did her best to attend frequent appointments, visit Luke, and keep herself from drowning. Serge continued to work.

The Family. Clinical encounters with the Leclairs, individually and together, often feature laughter and tears. They are a family that has faced a significant onslaught of mental illness and relative chaos in their lives in the span of four years. In addition to dealing with severe mental illness in two of their three children, they have had "normal" developmental dynamics to navigate through, between teenaged siblings, parental job losses and change, and moving. Crises and chaos swirled and swelled at various times, but did not ever stop. They were left always waiting for "the next thing," and then Luke's manic episode with psychosis seemed to completely shift the balance such that it was difficult to find solid ground again. Sometimes it seemed like they did not know how to go on. They are individually remarkable and talented people, and as a family they have found ways to tap into their individual strengths to find strength for the group. They will continue to face adversity and challenges over the next several years, and it will be important for them all to cultivate as many resources and supports as possible to keep filling their tank of resilience to keep fighting.

Snowfall

A substance that appears to dissipate in your
hands,
See it Fall,
Hear the children it brings,
Smell the warm soups in the air,
Taste the moisture in the wind,

As a snowflake tickles the tip of your nose,
The chills whisper in your ear,
Your eyelashes cling together from vapor,
With each and every step you leave behind,

A crunch, crunch follows like biting into an
apple,
The snowflakes blow you kisses,
The sunlight shines off the snow,
Making it look like it's winking at you,

So, do not blink or you'll miss it,
Don't dilly-dally now,
The snow awaits,
Making you appreciate the warmth,

Hinting there's still time for global warming to
cease,
Regulating the temperature of the earth's surface,
Drip, drip, as it seeps into rivers providing our
waters.

—Josée Leclair

CONCLUSION

When you hear a siren, it's easy to be alarmed and focus on the fact that someone is hurt or some sort of disaster is occurring. However, if you shift your perspective to the idea that a siren means that selfless, heroic people are racing to help someone in trouble, sirens come to represent hope and salvation. All that's required is to turn fear to hope. In the life of my family, alarm bells have often rung. But every time they have, professionals, family, friends, and God have responded to the call, rushing to our side to assist our family in our time of crisis.

> *Do not fear, for I have redeemed you; I have summoned you by name; you are mine. When you pass through the waters, I will be with you; and when you pass through the rivers, they will not sweep over you. When you walk through the fire, you will not be burned; the flames will not set you ablaze.*
> —Isaiah 43:1–2, NIV

> *See, I have engraved you on the palms of my hands; your walls are ever before me.*
> —Isaiah 49:16, NIV

> *You keep track of all my sorrows. You have collected all my tears in your bottle. You have recorded each one in your book.*
> —Psalm 56:8, NLT

These verses offer hope that God comforts and protects us and can use and redeem any circumstances in our lives, however difficult, challenging, or unimaginable.

Woven throughout what may seem like the random recollections of thoughts and experiences in this book are threads of hope that together create a wonderful masterpiece—for each place, person, and event has been constructed for such a time as this, to make a solid foundation that has kept our family grounded when everything else seemed to be falling apart.

Appendix A RESOURCES

Security blankets are the supports that help us get through a crisis to a place of stability. They come in various forms. Make sure you have them.

This is not an exhaustive list. Rather, it's a list of services we personally utilized.

Financial Resources

Did you know that if you have a formal diagnosis and are receiving treatment, you may be eligible for the federal Disability Tax Credit? To find out more, talk to a financial advisor and/or your doctor and have them fill out the paperwork. If you live in Ontario and you or your loved one is eighteen or older, you may also be eligible for the Ontario Disability Support Program. This helps finance the cost of dental, prescription medication, and room and board. Other provinces may have similar programs.

Another potential source of financial aid to explore is a Registered Disability Support Program. This is similar to an RRSP, only it provides your loved one with a disability pension.

If you are the caregiver of a child under the age of eighteen, be aware that Employment insurance has an income supplement called Parents of a Critically Ill Child, should you need be off work in order to care for your loved one. In addition, the EI sick benefit can help you care for your own medical needs.

It's important to know your employee benefit plans and check to see if you are eligible for any sub-plan top-ups while receiving EI.

Circle of Care

Make friends and invest in community. Don't wait for a crisis to make social connections. Find people with whom you have one or more things in common and build bridges. This will help others, and it will help you; it may serve as a lifeline when life beats you down. Get up, get out, and depend on your friends—not to do life for you, but to do life with you.

Medical Professionals

Ideally, you will want all of the below professionals to work in tandem, being aware of each other's role and course of treatment to avoid oversights or duplication of services.

Psychiatrist. Get one, preferably a good one. This will mean different things to different people, but ultimately you need someone you trust and who can be a resource for you. Ideally you want them to include loved ones in your care, such as a parent or partner if and as need be.

Counsellor. The same principles apply. Research states that treatment works best in combination with medication and therapy. Don't be afraid to ask questions about your therapist's training and level of competence for treatment. Remember: your ability to trust your counsellor and believe that they are a valuable resource is much more important than any credentials they may have.

Family Doctor. Find one you are comfortable with who is trained in mental health and comfortable prescribing medication. Shockingly, not all medical doctors are. One time when Josée was in crisis, her family doctor had no knowledge of the admittance process to a psych ward. We left that appointment and went directly to the hospital. Upon being transferred by hospital staff to the CAIP unit, Josée's family doctor's assistant called to inform us of the process, after taking the time to research it. Josée found another family doctor after that, as she had lost faith in that one.

Psychologist. Psychologists provide assessments and diagnoses. Note that psychologists provide the gold standard for the assessment and diagnosis of ADHD because of their standardized tools. This is different than a psychiatric assessment, although both are acceptable.

Mental Health and Addictions Nurse. These nurses are assigned to you following inpatient treatment, and if you live in Ontario they can be accessed through a Community Care Access Centre (CCAC).

Social Worker. Social workers are assigned during inpatient treatment and/or outpatient follow-up.

Specific Services

Note that the following services and organizations are those we used, and are specific to our province and community. You may need to research similar services and organizations in the province or community where you live.

Here 24/7. This Ontario hotline (1-844-437-3247, www.here247. ca) is a gateway service to all mental-health-related supports and referrals. What makes them distinct is that, although they don't provide counselling services per se, they provide crisis, intake, and support coordination services.

The following are some examples of the services offered: crisis workers, who can provide safety planning and risk and crisis assessment; support coordinators, who can provide a general assessment, arrange specific referrals, and place people on wait lists; the mobile crisis unit, which can visit persons on site when deemed appropriate; and the Family Education Program, an eight-week program geared towards adult caregivers.

Child and Adolescent Inpatient Program. The CAIP at the Grand River General Hospital offers a child and adolescent inpatient mental health unit at its Kitchener-Waterloo campus at 835 King Street West in Kitchener. It's an inpatient mental health unit providing care for children and youth seventeen years or younger, and admissions are coordinated through the hospital ER. CAIP has thirteen beds and accommodate short stays for patients who have difficulty functioning or participating in day-to-day routines and require the safety and intensity of a hospital admission. The unit includes a secure observation area for those who need the highest level of care in a safe environment.[17]

---

17 For more information, see the CAIP website: http://www.grhosp.on.ca/care/services-departments/mental-health-addiction/child-and-adolescent-inpatient-mental-health

The Parkwood Institute. Parkwood includes an adolescent psychiatry program that offers consultation and research. The program "provides specialized consultation, education, assessment, treatment, stabilization, and community integration services to adolescents between the ages of 13 and 18 living in Southwestern Ontario, who are experiencing serious mental illness that may be complicated by their developmental stage and/or concurrent diagnoses."[18] The consultation and outreach team "serves youth aged thirteen to eighteen by providing specialized therapeutic support such as psychotherapy, social skills training, group therapy, psychiatric consultation, family therapy, education and prevention, standard psychological testing, and school based support."[19]

The Ronald McDonald House. The mission of the Ronald McDonald house is to offer accommodations for the out-of-town families of hospitalized children with serious injuries. Rates are extremely affordable, and no family is turned away for lack of financial means. Their goal is to make sure that families are supported during times of crisis.[20]

* * *

If you are struggling or concerned about your mental health, I suggest that you talk to your pastor, doctor, or counsellor.

If you or someone you know is in crisis, you can call services such as Here 24/7 at 1-844-437-3247 or go to your local hospital's emergency department.

If you suspect someone is at risk, call the police for a wellness check. If you suspect they are at risk of imminent harm, call 911.

For more information about specific programs and services, contact the Canadian Mental Health Association or call directory assistance.

---

18 *St. Joseph's Health Care London,* "Mental Health Care: Adolescent Psychiatry Program." Date of access: August 19, 2018 (https://www.sjhc.london.on.ca/mental-health-care/programs-and-services/adolescent-psychiatry-program).

19 Ibid.

20 For more information, see the Ronald McDonald house website: https://www.rmhc-canada.ca/

If you need help as a caregiver, I highly recommend the *Here to Help* workbook, available as a free download here: http://www.heretohelp.bc.ca/workbook/family-self-care-and-recovery-from-mental-illness

Appendix B **INSPIRATIONS, ASPIRATIONS, AND AFFIRMATIONS**

The following are comments from students and staff at one high school where my daughters and I shared our story.

I appreciated the solid message of hope given throughout the presentation.

I learned that it is important to go to a caring adult in the school if I have a problem or if one of my friends is having a problem.

I loved to hear people my age talk instead of only adults.

I loved the way that there was at least one person from the family that everyone in the audience could identify with.

It was easy to connect with all of the family members.

I liked when the mother spoke the second time because she sounded more like a mom.

I especially appreciated the honesty of the mother about her daughter not going to her in her crisis.

I appreciated hearing from a family who is not perfect. My mom suffers from mental illness and is on medication. But she does not always take it so when I get up every morning I have no idea what I am getting up to. Hearing the family talk about their struggles made me feel better about my life because all of my friends seem to have perfect families. Now I feel like my family is ok.

Jane, the school's guidance counsellor, also wrote a very positive note:

Several grade 9's met me in the hallway at noon after thee assemblies and we visited a bit. All 3 boys commented on how they learned a lot at the assembly, how having a family there made it more interesting, and how they had no idea we had child and youth workers or a social worker in the building.

Several students self-referred to guidance for help later in the day.

One supply teacher present went to our VP at the end of the day to say how moved she was at the assembly and commended the school for planning such an opportunity for our students, as well as complimented your family for agreeing to come and speak.

All staff on the Wellness Team expressed awe and appreciation for the three of us and our willingness to take the risk to openly speak to a high school group.

Both students and staff commented on how amazed they were regarding the positive behaviour during both assemblies: "You could have heard a pin drop in both of the assemblies, so obviously the students present seemed engaged and respectful of the sharing."

Thanks so much to all 3 of you for your part in making our first-ever Mental Health Assembly and Wellness Week a true success at KCI. With deepest gratitude for your willingness to take a huge risk and be real surrounded by a room full of strangers. Know that your time at KCI has been impressionable and has made an incredible difference! God bless you as you journey on from here!

Appendix C LUKE'S COPING TECHNIQUES

Customize a Coping Tool Kit with self-soothing strategies for anxiety and emotional regulation. Remember to have it accessible at home and/or at school. The following are some ideas of things to include:

+ Grounding objects such as a photograph, rubbing stone, weighted stuffed animals, or essential oils, etc.
+ Breathing techniques
+ Imagery scripts for visualization and calming
+ Cue cards with positive thinking statements
+ Fidget toys such as squeezy balls, spinners, clickers, etc.
+ Distraction activities such as Zen tangles, mandalas, colouring pages, books, knitting, sparkle jars, etc.
+ Tapping techniques and cross lateral exercises
+ Yoga poses
+ Safety plan
+ Resource list of emergency names and numbers
+ Chewing gum or candy
+ Journal
+ Feeling cards
+ Relaxation techniques
+ Options card for coping with intense emotions
+ Head phones and favourite play list of music

- Apps like: Virtual Hope Box and/or Headspace amongst others that include distraction, visualization, inspiration, relaxation, and coping cards
- Schedule of daily activities
- For younger kids Kelso's choice wheel of problem solving skills
- Letter to yourself with personal encouragement

The possibilities are endless, so be sure to include what works. The internet is also a great resource for additional ideas.

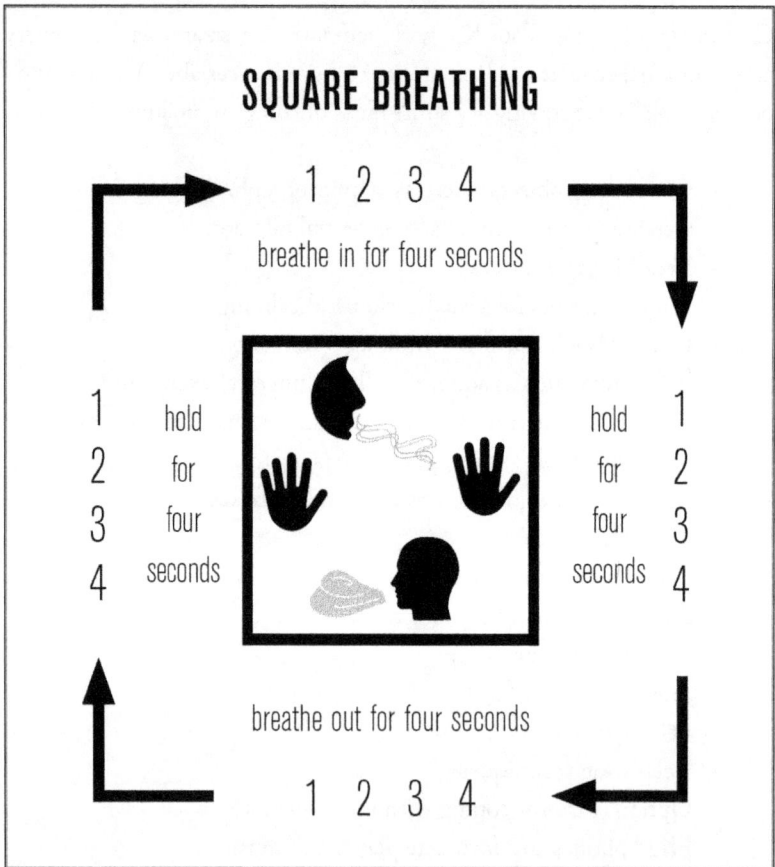

SQUARE BREATHING

1 2 3 4

breathe in for four seconds

1 hold   hold 1
2 for   for 2
3 four   four 3
4 seconds   seconds 4

breathe out for four seconds

1 2 3 4

ABOUT
THE
AUTHOR

Melody Leclair is a first-time author and registered psychotherapist. She obtained her first degree in 1998 from Emmanuel Bible College and graduated with a Bachelor of Religious Education in Counselling Studies. Fifteen years later, in 2013, she complemented it with a Master of Spiritual Care and Psychotherapy from Wilfrid Laurier University, fulfilling a life-long dream and receiving an Excellence Award. Melody has worked as a counsellor in both private practice and, currently, within an agency setting. She is also an accomplished public speaker who speaks to various issues of mental health and shares passionately from professional and personal perspectives. Her family has been known to accompany her and speak from their lived experiences.

Melody lives in Ontario with her husband Serge and their three children, Josée, Karina, and Luke. Since first meeting her husband, their marriage has been full of adventures. She enjoys family camping near and far and even has some tales of camping with bears. Her faith in God and her community of friends and family are constant sources of strength and resilience for her.

To connect with Melody or book her for a speaking engagement, please visit whenlightningstrikestwice.com.

The Leclair family.
Photo credit: Laurie Goodman.

www.ingramcontent.com/pod-product-compliance
Lightning Source LLC
Chambersburg PA
CBHW061041110426
42740CB00050B/2638